HOW TO WRITE MAGAZINE ARTICLES THAT SELL

HOW TO WRITE MAGAZINE ARTICLES THAT SELL

W. P. WILLIAMS AND
JOSEPH VAN ZANDT

Contemporary Books, Inc.
Chicago

Library of Congress Cataloging in Publication Data

Williams, W. P., 1953-
   How to write magazine articles that sell.

   Includes index.
   1. Authorship.   I. Van Zandt, Joseph,
1940-   joint author. II. Title.
PN147.W534   1979   808'.025   78-23606
ISBN 0-8092-7382-9
ISBN 0-8092-7381-0 pbk.

Copyright © 1979 by W. P. Williams and Joseph Van Zandt
All rights reserved
Published by Contemporary Books, Inc.
180 North Michigan Avenue, Chicago, Illinois 60601
Manufactured in the United States of America
Library of Congress Catalog Card Number:
International Standard Book Number: 0-8092-7382-9 (cloth)
                                                0-8092-7381-0 (paper)

Published simultaneously in Canada by
Beaverbooks
953 Dillingham Road
Pickering, Ontario L1W 1Z7
Canada

Contents

Introduction *vii*

Part I Planning the Article 1
1 Who Buys Magazine Articles? *3*
2 Developing Article Ideas *9*
3 Research *19*

Part II Writing the Article 27
4 Flair and Style *29*
5 Photojournalism *47*

Part III Selling Your Articles 53
6 Making Contact *55*
7 Legal Matters *63*
8 Getting "into the Business" *75*
9 The Bottom Line *81*

Conclusion *87*

Appendix *89*

Index *95*

Introduction

The world of the free-lance writer, like that of the private eye or the Wild West cowboy, conjures up a wide variety of images—all of them exciting and adventurous. In fact, real-life cowboys and private detectives lead rather mundane lives with few exceptions. After all, what's so exciting about looking at the tail end of a herd of steers or bird-dogging errant spouses day after day?

The free-lance writer faces his share of drudgery, too, especially one who does it as his sole source of income. Banging out stories on a typewriter hour after hour is no picnic. But despite the occasional tedium, the world of the free-lance writer really is an interesting, exciting, and adventurous place.

Free-lance writers earn money in many ways, from preparing speeches to handling publicity for individuals and organizations to producing fiction—short stories and novels. But the vast majority of free-lance writers earn their living by writing for magazines of various types. Why? Because with more than three thousand magazines across the country, the potential for selling articles is virtually limitless.

Perhaps you already earn your living in a related field—as a newspaper reporter, a radio or TV news writer, a PR man. Or perhaps you are a secretary, and your creative writing is limited to preparing business letters that the boss is too busy for. Even if your writing has been limited to term papers and theses in high school or college, you can make it writing articles for magazines—*if* you really want to.

The only requirements are: (a) a working knowledge of conversational English (leave the polysyllabic doubletalk to the Ph.D.s); (b) reasonable skill as a typist (whether you use the "hunt and peck" method or more orthodox approach is unimportant); and (c) the ability to sell your stuff.

If you possess the first two of these three requirements, take heart, because the purpose of this book is to help you achieve number three. And, after all, no matter how exciting the world of the free-lancer is, and no matter that it provides you with instant status (no foolin'—just drop the fact that you are a writer at the next party you attend and see how fast you attract a doting crowd of your very own groupies), the bottom line is money.

Money pays for all of your various expenses (expensive dinners with contacts, all that travel, phone calls, and the like). Hopefully, it will also pay for things like the rent and your car payment. And last of all, it is the single best criterion for gauging your success as a free-lance magazine writer—the best writers earn the most money. It's like the time someone asked millionaire J. Paul Getty why he got such a kick out of winning a few dollars playing poker. His reply: "Despite my wealth, money remains the single best way of keeping score."

So, whether your goal as a free-lance magazine writer is to make it your sole profession, or whether you prefer to stay in your current career and just dabble in article writing as a hobby, the best way to keep score is with the money you earn.

No matter how many hundreds of magazine articles you do in the years ahead, every single one requires three basic steps, and these steps are represented in the three sections of this book:

1. Planning the article
2. Writing the article
3. Selling the article

With that as an introduction, let's get on with the business of helping you to become a successful writer of articles for magazines.

part I

Planning the Article

1

Who Buys Magazine Articles?

The question of who buys magazine articles really isn't a stupid one. The obvious answer is magazine editors, of course. But what we're getting at here is what kinds of magazines. With three thousand-plus magazines out there looking for fresh material every month, your chances of selling every article you write are great indeed, *if* you know where to find the right one.

Types of Magazines

A magazine can be categorized in many ways—by the type of audience it reaches, by the scope of its circulation, by the physical characteristics of the product, and by the approach it takes, among other things.

Tabloid Versus Slick Magazines

A slick magazine is one that is printed on glossy, coated stock. It usually has a four-color cover and a number of full-color ads and layouts inside. Most of the magazines you are familiar with are this type—*Playboy, Time, Sports Illustrated, Ms.,* and others.

Because of the high cost of coated stock plus the need to print on heat-dry presses, the slick magazine is almost always a standard size (8½ x 11 trim size or thereabouts). A few tabloid-size slick magazines still exist, but for the most part they are trade publications rather than consumer magazines like those found on the newsstand.

The tabloid magazines vary in dimensions but are usually similar in size and appearance to such publications as *Rolling Stone, Country Style,* and *Sporting News.*

The tabloid magazines are usually printed on newsprint (the same type of stock as your daily papers). Their content tends to be more timely than the slick magazines, and their style is usually more relaxed and casual. In many respects, the tabloid magazines are actually a cross between the newspaper and the slick magazine.

Tabloid magazines usually (but not always) pay less per article than the slicks, and they tend to be less demanding as well. Finally, since they don't need early deadlines (at least as early as the slicks), you can sell a story that you may stumble across at the last minute easier to a tabloid magazine than a slick magazine.

Regional Versus National Magazines

Most of the magazines you are familiar with are nationally circulated. That means their content must be such that it appeals to people in Mississippi as well as Maine. But while the nationally circulated magazines are the best known, the vast majority of magazines are regionally circulated and written for the people in a particular city or section of the country.

For example, many states produce their own "state" magazines, often subsidized with tax money, to promote tourism. (*Arizona Highways* is generally considered the best of the state magazines.) Then there are the new so-called "city" magazines, such as *New York* and *Chicago.* These are not subsidized but do help promote a city anyway, even though they often carry articles of a negative nature.

Other types of regionally circulated magazines include those dealing with hobbies and sports. For example, although there are just two nationally circulated ski magazines, there are some fifteen regionally circulated magazines for skiers. Each offers its readers news and features that can't be found in the major magazines.

Vertical Versus Horizontal Magazines

Horizontal magazines can be slick or tabloid, regional or national in circulation. What makes them different from so-called vertical magazines is that they produce an editorial product that appeals to a wide variety of people; the vertical magazine, on the other hand, is aimed at a highly specific reader. For example, *Arizona Highways* is a horizontal magazine because it has appeal for all kinds of people—young and old, male and female, blue collar worker and executive. *Skate Boarder,* on the other hand, while nationally circulated, is a vertical book because it appeals just to those people who are interested in the sport of skateboarding and no others.

Large Versus Small Circulation

While regional magazines tend to have smaller circulations than nationally circulated publications, this is not always true. For example, *Chicago* magazine is a regional book but has a circulation of more than a hundred thousand. *Water*

Skier magazine, on the other hand, has national distribution, but its circulation is less than ten thousand.

The magazine's circulation has a great bearing on the amount of money it can pay for articles. Obviously, a magazine with ten thousand circulation can't pay the kind of money that *Playboy* can for the same article.

Trade Versus Consumer

Consumer magazines are those sold on newsstands and magazine racks. They are written for the entertainment of some or all of the public at large. Trade magazines are written specifically for use by people who work in a particular field—in this sense they are vertical publications. An example of a trade magazine would be *Advertising Age*.

Profit Versus Nonprofit Magazines

A lot of magazines are nonprofit, but only some of them are meant to be that way. What we mean by nonprofit magazines are those produced by nonprofit organizations as a means of informing members of vital information or as a means of building membership. Examples are magazines such as the *Kiwanian,* the *Rotarian,* the *Princeton Tiger,* and the *Daughters of the American Revolution*.

While such magazines tend to pay less than "for-profit" magazines for articles, this is not always the case. The *Legionnaire,* for example, pays quite well.

Who Buys What

Breaking down the many magazines by types is essential to helping you zero in on those that are most likely to buy a particular article from you. But with three thousand or so magazines from which to choose, you now must know where to go to find the potential buyers of your work.

The Directories

Just as you would use the telephone book to look up the phone number of a friend, directories are also available for looking up magazines by field of interest. While none of these offers a complete listing of all magazines, you can cover a good deal of ground quickly by referring to them.

One of the most comprehensive of the directories is the *N.W. Ayer Directory*. It lists newspapers and magazines throughout the United States and Canada, giving addresses, names of key editors, and type of material carried.

Other excellent reference guides are the Standard Rate and Data Service directories. They publish one for consumer magazines, another for business publications, and a third for farm publications. The SRDS publications are not sold in book shops, but you can sometimes find them in libraries. Your best source, however, is an advertising agency. Since the SRDS directories are updated every month, you can sometimes get an old one just by writing or asking for one from a local ad agency. (Or write to SRDS, 5201 Old Orchard Road, Skokie, Illinois 60051.)

If you have an article to sell that may have appeal to newspapers as well as magazines, you can get a complete listing of daily and weekly papers across the country in the *Editor and Publisher Yearbook*. Most libraries carry the E & P yearbook. Or you can write for one to Editor and Publisher, 570 Lexington Avenue, New York, New York 10017.

Another excellent source of magazines that purchase articles is *Writer's Market*. This book is updated yearly and can be obtained at most book stores as well as at most libraries.

We also suggest you consider subscribing to one or both of the magazines aimed at free-lance writers such as yourself—the *Writer* and *Writer's Digest*. Both are nationally circulated and are sold on most big city newsstands as well as carried in many libraries. Both carry regular listings of magazines that are looking for specific types of stories, as well as occasional "inside tips" on hot markets.

Last but not least, use the *Reader's Guide to Periodical Literature* at your friendly local library. It lists articles by subject matter, so you simply look up various headings that could apply to an article you have in mind. This will give you an idea of which magazines may be interested in it as well as what has already been published on the subject, so that you can take a fresh approach.

Develop a Magazine File

As you go about the business of checking for various magazines that might be interested in your articles, we suggest you type up a 3 x 5 card for each, listing the names of the magazine, its address, phone number, and names of key editors. Then file the cards alphabetically, by subject matter.

If you write to one and get an interesting reply, make a note of it on the back of your card, along with the date of the correspondence. The editor may have declined your story offer but suggested another possibility. Or he may have said he's not looking for any articles. Whatever he says, your notations will save you time and effort later on.

2

Developing Article Ideas

How many times have you heard someone say, "He owes it all to me. I gave him the idea in the first place"?

In the case of magazine articles, a good idea is an absolute prerequisite for a good article. But what you do with the idea is every bit as important when it comes to selling your work.

An old saying goes, "Success is 2 percent inspiration, 98 percent perspiration." Believe it, it's true! Once you have the germ of an idea, you have to stretch it in every direction to see if it holds up under scrutiny and to determine if it can be expanded. It takes a certain spark of creativity to take the basic idea from its embryonic stage to finished article.

The mark of the professional writer is his ability to detect something in a subject that no one else has thought of before (or at least written about before). Top feature writers have a sixth sense—old-time newspaper reporters call it a "nose for news." Implied here is a certain aggressiveness in seeking out story possibilities. Don't believe all the movie baloney about being inspired at 2 A.M. and jumping up from a sound sleep to write it all down while it's fresh in your mind. Writers who wait around for a bolt of lightning tend to get very hungry.

Writers need concentration and discipline. You have to be able to sit down at the typewriter and grind it out, even when you'd rather be playing tennis. As a free-lance writer, you don't have an editor or boss to hold your nose to the grindstone. The only person who will force you to keep at it is you. If you happen to be out of ideas, the best way to find some is to start hunting for them.

List Your Likes and Interests

Neophytes in this business of free-lance writing make the mistake of going after stories about which they know nothing. For example, the guy who failed high school chemistry suddenly decides to do an in-depth story about water pollution. The kid who won his only high school letter on the debating team decides he's going to interview Mean Joe Greene of the Pittsburgh Steelers.

Can they get their story? Heck, yes, but it is a sure thing that it won't be easy. Since the name of the game (or at least the best way of keeping score) is the money you earn, doesn't it make more sense to produce two or three salable articles about subjects you know and understand than to struggle to produce one on a subject that you know little or nothing about, and perhaps dislike as well?

When a person decides to start a business, the first thing he should do is to prepare a pro forma (or business plan). It not only is used as a guideline for developing his idea but also helps him to get financing from the bank.

The magazine writer needs something similar, but in his case it should be a concise list of his likes, interests, and areas of expertise. Each item in the list should be ranked according to its relative potential for producing stories (that's stories, not story). Whenever you are at a loss for a story idea, fall back on your list of likes and interests—it's bound to give you some material.

Make a habit of visiting your local library on a regular basis. Don't look for a specific book, but just roam the aisles and stacks. If you spot a book that looks interesting, pull it out and scan it. Carry a notebook and pen, and whenever you get a good idea, jot it down. And don't be afraid to take an armful of books home. Some people think that to be a "legitimate" writer, everything you produce must be 100 percent fresh and original. Not so. Most successful writers borrow liberally from each other. (Just make sure you don't plagiarize, or lift material word for word without quoting your source. In the case of copyrighted material, get permission to use it.)

Look Close to Home

Just about the very first thing students in creative writing classes hear is to stick to subjects they are familiar with. Mark Twain wrote about life on the Mississippi because that was his life. In many ways he was Tom Sawyer and Huck Finn together. Joseph Conrad wrote about the sea because he had actually been a merchant sailor, and that was the life he knew. Ernest Hemingway wrote about man's struggle with nature because he lived that life as a soldier of fortune, hunter, and fisherman.

Does that mean you are out of luck if your background doesn't involve some equally flamboyant or dangerous environment? Of course not. We've all had plenty of interesting events in our lives—the trick is to spot them and then describe them in a way that others can relate to.

And besides, you aren't setting out to write the Great American Novel, just to produce interesting, salable articles for magazines. So that makes your task much easier.

Nonetheless, you will have your best luck in developing

article ideas close to home, where you are familiar, and where gathering information will be relatively easy.

Just as you developed a list of likes and interests, we suggest you take a few days to reexplore your neighborhood, town, and locale. Really take a look at things instead of just blasting along on the freeway. In fact, try a walking or bike-riding tour instead of using your car. Carry a camera, and take photos of everything that strikes you in any way. And take copious notes. Later you can sift and sort everything out, discarding the obviously bad possibilities and filing the better ideas for future reference.

And think positive. Don't think that because you live in a small, out-of-the-way town that there won't be anything interesting to write about. Likewise, if you come from a major city, don't assume that it has already been picked to death by other writers.

For example, we happen to live in Chicago. This city has two daily papers, dozens of neighborhood and ethnic papers, forty radio stations, and a half dozen TV stations. It has scores of authors and professional writers, all of whom use this city for story fodder day in and day out.

But, as poet Carl Sandburg observed, Chicago is a city that is constantly undergoing death and rebirth, with each new generation, with each change of season, with each new family that arrives. We tend not to notice it in our day-to-day existence, but a study of two photos of the same location ten years apart will show major changes in almost every instance.

As we look from my office window, we can see all kinds of story possibilities. The lake off in the distance—where is it in terms of water quality compared with a few years ago? How about the much-heralded planting of salmon and trout— where is the program now, and how does its future look? What about the nuclear power plant up in Zion? Have there been problems with nuclear waste leaks? Is the coolant water causing problems in the lake? The harbor a few blocks away is overflowing with pleasure boats. Is that the case elsewhere on the Great Lakes? Is the mooring shortage also a problem elsewhere, such as on each coast, as well?

The building next door, formerly a high-rise apartment complex, has been converted to a condominium development. In fact, the condo conversion boom shows no sign of a letup. It is a natural for a magazine story.

Outside the temperature is a chilly fifty degrees, even though it is summertime. How is Chicago faring in terms of climate changes? Do the big buildings really cause changes in climate?

Well, enough of this. The point is that without so much as leaving our office, we can see countless possibilities for magazine articles all around us. Imagine how many more we could find by getting out into the neighborhoods and talking with people.

Use Newspapers and Magazines

Some of the best sources for article ideas are publications of all types. Subscribe to as many as possible. (Remember to deduct the cost. As a writer, you are entitled to write off all such costs as part of your necessary research.) If you can't afford to subscribe to a lot of publications, read as many as possible at the library, and when you come across an interesting article, Xerox it or take notes from it for future reference.

Start a separate file with clippings and notes on various article possibilities.

Perhaps the best sources of ideas are those little blurbs or fillers all newspapers use. You may see a mere paragraph about an interesting subject, but it could be enough to get you started on an idea for an article of your own.

Get on Everyone's Mailing List

As a free-lance writer you will have little trouble getting your name added to various mailing lists. Virtually every large company has its own public relations staff, whose main function is to get favorable publicity for the company. The way this is done is by sending out news releases and photos on a regular basis to newspapers, magazines, radio and TV stations, *and* to writers such as yourself who may use the material in a column or future feature article.

In addition to companies, many other organizations also have public relations and publicity people who crank out news releases and arrange for interviews of key people with writers such as you. These organizations include high schools and colleges, fraternal and civic organizations, political parties, and a wide variety of special interest groups, trade organizations, and similar bodies.

The press releases always give a name and phone number of someone to contact for more information. So if you hit on something that has possibilities, you can often get everything you need for your article with a single phone call or appointment.

We suggest you get a post office box. Otherwise, your mailman may have fits trying to get all your daily mail into your home box. As for sifting through everything each day, you'll discover that it is not nearly as time-consuming as you might think. Generally, most press releases carry headlines that announce the contents. By scanning these, you can determine which releases require a full reading, which should be discarded, and which should be filed for future use.

Developing the Idea

So far, we've gone into detail to help you come up with story ideas. The next step is to develop that idea. Every story possibility can be approached from a wide variety of angles. (Old-time editors will tell you that if you give ten writers the same basic material, they will come up with ten distinct stories.)

Questions such as how to begin and wrap the article up,

what material is relevant and what should be excluded, and what is the main thrust (or theme) of the article must be answered. Determining these things will tell you in what direction to go in researching the article further. You may find as you proceed that your original idea requires expansion, or you may find that alternate ideas crop up that are more interesting than your original idea. Stay flexible, and don't be afraid to "change horses in the middle of the stream." To do otherwise would be to invite the possibility of "choking" your story.

On the other hand, don't let yourself become sidetracked with unrelated material. Pursuing unrelated research is a waste of time.

Always keep in mind where your research is taking you, and go in that direction. Preliminary research should zero in on the main points you want to cover. Preliminary research should also provide the deciding factor that tells you whether or not the original idea is worth pursuing further. Often what seems like a good idea for an article washes out. If this occurs, don't be afraid to drop the idea.

Your next decision must be whether enough information is available to make your idea into an interesting article. Good feature articles don't repeat and aren't padded with what editors call fluff.

Is your idea fresh? If someone else has already published an article on the subject, is there still room for another article without simply rehashing the first one? If the first article didn't do a complete job of reporting the key facts, there is still a chance for you to do a better and more concise job. Articles can always be updated with new facts and expanded to cover details not previously mentioned, but don't assume that a few new facts of little importance will reawaken the interest of the reader (and the editor).

Always compare your article idea with other articles on the same subject. Suppose you are the editor who is asked to evaluate your article for use in a given magazine. Would you buy it?

And just because a subject may appear earthshaking to you, that doesn't mean it will be equally important to others. If in doubt, go to people who will be objective and honest with you about the article. Do *not* ask your family or close friends—they will encourage you no matter what. If you can't get others interested in your idea, chances are it's not so hot after all.

Next ask yourself if your ideas for the article are based on cold facts or your own opinions. Unless you are a philosophical genius, it is doubtful that many others will really care all that much about how you feel about the subject. Your role as writer is to gather pertinent information on a subject and then report it in a clear and concise way. If you can't support your position with facts, chances are you are too emotionally involved in the subject matter to do a good job of reporting on it.

Don't tread in waters that are unknown to you and beyond your level of comprehension. If you don't understand your subject, it will come across to your reader immediately.

Understanding a subject also gives you a well-rounded view of what should be included to make your article a complete package. Don't underestimate your own experiences and stored knowledge. Most good feature writers eventually become authorities in one or more areas.

Even if your idea for an article has wide interest, don't pursue it unless you are interested in it yourself as well. If a topic seems dull to you, it will be difficult to write about it enthusiastically. Sure, you can struggle through with the idea, but why subject yourself to this sort of mental torture when there are hundreds of other more appealing ideas for you to work on. Not liking the subject from the start should be enough to keep you from doing it altogether.

The Final Test

If everything seems to check out positively for a go-ahead on the story, here's a final test before you proceed:

Write a synopsis of your idea, stating all the facts and information that you have uncovered. If you are then satisfied, send out queries along with the synopsis to several magazine editors to see if they feel the same way.

A positive response to your query will tell you that your idea has merit. But don't let a single negative reply sour you. You may be surprised when a different editor writes back and asks you to submit the article.

If an editor doesn't like your idea, don't expect him to write back and give you a detailed explanation of why he doesn't like it. Editors get scores of queries each month. Chances are if your story idea bombs, you'll simply receive a form letter advising you that the magazine in question is not interested in the idea. This is not a personal rebuke, and it should in no way deter you from suggesting other ideas to that same publication or from submitting the same idea to other magazines.

3

Research

Your ultimate success as a free-lance magazine writer will depend on how well you research your subjects. No matter how good your story idea, without the facts to back up what you want to get across, it will fail. Learning how to get the necessary information and other facts to substantiate what you are trying to prove is an involved process.

An inexperienced writer with a marvelous idea may produce a dud of an article without proper research, while a seasoned pro with an ordinary idea may produce a stunning piece with the aid of proper research.

A writer must know not only where to go but how to go about collecting background information. In fact, the good researcher will more likely face a problem of overabundance of information than lack of it. That's why you have to constantly keep in mind the aim of your article and avoid tracking down apparently interesting information that really isn't directly related to your subject matter.

We don't advocate a speed-reading course, but you definitely should master the art of skimming over books and other materials so that you can cover the maximum amount of ground in the minimum length of time.

Libraries

Perhaps your greatest single source of background information is the library, both public and others (professional, college, and private). Your greatest single source of references should be the *Reader's Guide to Periodical Literature,* which lists all articles that have appeared in magazines.

Check the publication dates of all articles listed to be sure that they are current and their material isn't dated. It won't do any good to take notes on an article that appeared ten years ago if it deals with a subject that has changed greatly. (For example, 35-mm cameras have undergone major changes in design, function, and size during the past ten years. What was true then is almost certainly outdated today.)

Also check the vertical files in the library for pamphlets and brochures that may relate to your subject matter. Also ask the librarian for additional information—many maintain their own files with newspaper and magazine clippings relating to a variety of topics.

Do not overlook other libraries, such as those of colleges and professional organizations as well as privately endowed libraries. Most of these will allow you to use their facilities if you request it. And in the case of researching highly technical subjects, you may not be able to find the information you need in public libraries.

Newspaper Morgues

All but the smallest community newspapers maintain their own reference libraries, which consist of files of clippings on virtually every subject reported on by the newspaper. In addition to clippings, newspaper libraries (the colloquial name is morgue) have extensive photo files plus microfilm strips of each issue, sometimes going back a hundred years or more.

Newspapers don't advertise their morgues as being open to the public, but in most cases you will be given permission to use the morgue if you explain to the editor and/or librarian that you are a free-lance writer.

Surveys

Many times you will discover that the information you need for your article simply isn't available from the usual sources. For example, suppose you are doing an article on changing attitudes toward premarital sex or smoking marijuana or another topical subject. One way of obtaining up-to-the-minute statistics is by conducting your own survey.

Before conducting your survey, you must decide exactly whom you wish to poll and what it is you wish to learn. Surveys may be conducted in person (door-to-door, on the street, etc.), by phone, or through the mail.

Generally, the shorter your survey, the more likely you will be to get good responses. Some surveys may consist of a single question, although chances are that if you limit your questions to a single page, you'll still get good response.

If you send your questionnaires out through the mail, be sure to include a stamped, addressed return envelope. This will greatly increase the responses. Also, if you want to survey a hundred people, send out two hundred questionnaires, figuring that some people will just not respond and others (such as teenagers) may fill the questionnaire out in an obviously erroneous manner.

Wording of the questions can affect the results of your survey, and entire college courses are given in just this kind of thing. Just make sure where your questions are leading and that they are simple and direct.

It is also a good idea to send a cover letter with your questionnaire explaining what the purpose of the survey is. Advise respondents that all information will be kept confidential, and unless absolutely necessary, don't ask for names or addresses on your questionnaire.

If your survey is of a highly specialized nature, try to get a mailing list that zeroes in on the people you want to reach. For example, if you are doing an article on teachers' attitudes, see if you can get several schools to send out or distribute your questionnaires for you.

Computerized mailing lists can be purchased from specialty direct mail houses, but since you are trying to make a profit on your article, you should avoid purchasing a list if possible. In most instances professional and other organizations will provide access to their lists if you can show them that you are a bona fide writer who will not abuse the access.

Contacting Experts

To give a firm base for the information in your article, it may be advisable to contact various experts and authorities. Readers find it much easier to believe material from someone they admire or respect than from a writer they have probably never heard of. Suppose, for example, that you are doing an article on the mystique of the Indianapolis 500-mile race. Think how much more impact your article would have if you were to include comments of top drivers such as A. J. Foyt and Mario Andretti in your report.

In the case of a controversial subject, contact experts on both sides and air their views. Not only is this the fair thing to do; it makes for the most interesting content as well.

Sometimes the experts may not be readily available. That's when your ingenuity comes into play. If you can't get through by phone, try a letter. If that fails, how about a Mailgram or a Telegram? If all else fails, you should be prepared to track the individual down and buttonhole him if at all possible.

Experienced reporters who come up against this kind of stonewalling use the subtle threat to get their foot in the door. They tell the expert's secretary or subordinate that unless they are able to talk to so-and-so, they'll have to run the story without his comments and that will result in a one-sided picture. Not only that, they'll have to say that so-and-so was unavailable for comment—and, of course, that puts a bad light on the individual.

When writing to an expert for an interview or answers to questions by letter, be sure to state specifically what you want and when you need the information. Some writers make a point of pushing their real deadline up a week or two, just in case they can't reach the source and they want to use the "urgent" ploy.

Contact Professional Organizations

When researching articles, don't overlook professional organizations in your search for information. Many times professional and other nonprofit organizations maintain elaborate files of material on subjects of interest to their members and/or the general public. This information is available, usually at no cost, and usually just for the asking.

For example, suppose you are working on a piece about vacationing in Michigan. By contacting the Michigan Tourist Council, you could receive a variety of maps, brochures, photos, lists, article reprints, and similar materials. And if the materials sent to you didn't answer all of your questions, a phone call to the office in Lansing would result in a staff member's rounding up the additional information for you.

When requesting photos, be specific in stating your exact needs, whether they be for black-and-white glossies or color transparencies (slides). Usually professional and other nonprofit organizations have extensive photo files, so be sure to get exactly what you need to illustrate your article; be specific in your request. In the case of doing an article on Michigan vacations, specify if you want photos of a particular city, of nature scenes, of sports activities, and the like.

You should remember that such organizations consider education of the public one of their prime aims. So when a free-lance magazine writer such as you contacts them for assistance, he can be sure that he will receive it.

In many instances you will find yourself researching a subject where a participating company or organization has a public relations agency representing its viewpoint. Such agencies' very existence depends on their ability to place articles in various publications on their own as well as through free-lance writers.

Many free-lance magazine writers are skeptical of public relations firms, but those of us who deal with such agencies regularly have learned that they can be of immeasurable help. Most of their personnel have journalism backgrounds and as such will be careful not to try to tell you how to write your article. But when requested, they will provide you with a detailed report, sometimes so well done it can actually be submitted in its entirety as your article. (We're not advising such a practice, just pointing out that it is possible.)

Building Your Own Files

The first thing a free-lance writer learns is to develop his own filing system. Any time you come across something that looks interesting, file it, especially if it relates to subjects you regularly write about.

If you are like most free-lance writers, you will not win any awards for your clerical and organizational skills. It is easy to just toss everything of interest into a drawer. But when it comes time to find an item you "filed" two or three months ago, you now must shuffle through your accumulated materials in hopes of retrieving the needed document or clipping.

Not only is time wasted but in the process your creative

mood tends to become deflated somewhat. The solution is obvious—set up a logical and orderly filing system now. Whether you file items alphabetically or by subject is up to you. But either way, you will have a much easier time retrieving materials.

A standard filing cabinet works best, with manila file folders used for storing items. You should also get a book case or shelf for filing large pamphlets, books, and other such materials. As you read various publications, be sure to make note of any offers of free literature that deals with subjects of interest to you. Then take a few minutes to write for the literature—you never can tell when it might be exactly what you need for a particular item or article.

One other thing—don't discard research materials after you use them in one article. Save them for possible use in similar or related articles at a later time. You should also retain such materials just in case someone questions your sources. (In the case of controversial articles, it is possible that you could become involved in litigation, in which case documentation of your charges is a must.)

part II

Writing the Article

4

Flair and Style

There is a myth about successful writers that maintains that to make it, you have to develop your own unique style of writing. In a word, that is bunk!

To be sure, the great authors of history did (and do) have style, but that's not necessarily the same as having "a style." A case can be made that the great authors did have their own unique styles; for example, Twain, Dickens, Hemingway, Fitzgerald. And we'll concede the point—up to a point.

In a word, perhaps a handful of writers among the thousands who have plied their trade can be instantly recognized for their style. As for the 99.9 percent of the remainder—many of whom became rich and famous—you would be hard put to distinguish their work from scores of others from their particular period. And when it comes to writers of magazine articles as opposed to the "true" authors of novels and plays, the need for a distinct personal style is even less important.

What is important is to produce articles that are easily understood, that deal with topics of interest at the time, and that conform to the requirements of the specific publication for which they are written. In other words, don't worry about developing a unique style as much as writing with style and flair. If you eventually become rich and famous and people can recognize your work at a glance, terrific. But don't get all hung up on the subject.

Get Organized

More important than developing a deathless style (at least when it comes to selling your work) is organizing your material properly. Collecting all the necessary information is half the battle. Presenting it properly is the other half. Both are essential for an interesting and compelling piece.

Facts are meaningless in an article unless they are linked together. Readers don't like to figure things out for themselves, at least in nonfiction articles. They expect the writer to put the pieces of the puzzle together for them. The key to doing this lies in selecting the right "slant," or approach.

Unfortunately, there is no formula or established method for determining the correct approach to a story. It is a skill that is developed only from experience, and by reading everything you can get your hands on to see how other writers approach various subjects.

There are several things we can advise you on in your writing. For one, don't make the reader guess what you mean. Spell it out. Second, if you have to opt for a forceful presentation as opposed to a sedate one, be forceful. That means give your articles impact. When the reader finishes your article, his reaction should be "Wow."

Proper organization of your material is what will get this kind of result.

Chronology

The easiest method for organizing your material is in chronological order. You tell about events as they happened, as long as they happened in an interesting manner. For the chronological approach to work, the story should build to a climax. This requires the writer to discard all facts that are not directly related, to avoid dwelling on the mundane, and to stick to the point.

The Interview

The interview is one of the most basic tools of the magazine writer. We aren't referring to the informal interviews that take place when a reporter buttonholes a source for a question or two. We mean the prearranged meeting of writer and source (or sources) during which the source submits to a variety of questions.

Such meetings produce material for a wide variety of articles, among which is the interview (second use). Interview articles are presented in several fashions, including the standard Q&A and the currently popular "Playboy-type interview," itself a variation of the Q&A. The third much-used type is that employed by people such as Rex Reed, where the questions and answers are woven into a type of short story, complete with all kinds of fiction-writing devices from detailed description to dialogue.

Regardless of your method of presenting the results of your interview, learning how to conduct one is vital to your success in selling magazine articles.

True, there is no single right or wrong approach. Some writers use a tape recorder, while others take notes and some simply commit the discussion to memory. Interviews can take place just about anywhere as well—the deck of a pitching boat, a noisy bowling alley, an executive's office, the golf course.

The key to a successful interview (one in which you come away with solid material for your article) lies in getting through to the real person to whom you are directing the questions.

The biggest barrier is the average person's distrust of writers and reporters. You may be doing an important service, but to the interviewee, you are invading his privacy. This attitude prevails not just with the man on the street but with public figures and celebrities as well.

To help win his confidence, advise the interviewee in advance about the type of questions you will be asking. Tell him where you intend to sell your article so he is aware in advance in what magazine it will appear. Send the person a few clippings of other articles you have written so that he can see for himself that you are not an ogre.

Then do some advance legwork. If the interviewee is well known, read up on him, taking notes so you will be able to remember as much about his views and activities as possible. And jot down his answers to pertinent questions asked by other interviewers.

Now when you actually get together for the interview, you can accomplish two things. First, you can ask questions of such a nature that your interviewee will be aware that you know a good deal about him—this will be flattering, even if he is a gangster. Second, you can avoid the mundane questions asked so often (you already have this information) and get down to the meat of the interview.

Have questions written down in case the conversation slows down or your mind goes blank for a moment. And remember that it is up to you to keep the conversation going in the direction you wish. Should you allow the interviewee to digress or veer off on a topic other than the one you are discussing? There is no definitive answer for this one. You have to let your instincts guide you and play it by ear. Sometimes your subject will suddenly open up in an area you least expected, so let him continue.

While some lucky writers are able to follow their subjects around for two or three days to observe them at their regular activities, this is not usually the case. The standard interview takes an hour or so, and if you blow it, there is no going back and asking for a second chance. You must get all the material you want during this single meeting.

Remember that you are there to interview, not merely to fill in the blanks for an article that is almost completed. People can sense when a writer does this, and it makes them edgy and hostile.

One of your objectives is to find out what the person in question is really like. Listen to what he is saying as well as what he is *not* saying. Is he trying to steer you away from a particular subject? If so, you must subtly steer the conversation back on course.

If you can somehow get to the heart of your subject, you will be able to get him talking about things that he's never mentioned before to anyone, and *that* is what separates the best interviewers from the also-rans.

When you hit on the "connection," you'll know it.

Try to save your most controversial question for last. Sometimes a person will be offended (or at least fake indignation) and end the interview then and there. At least now you have plenty of good material already. A good way to deal with touchy subjects is to quote what another person said and then ask your own subject to respond. In this way, you don't come across like you are giving your own opinions.

To TAPE OR NOT TO TAPE. There are essentially three methods for conducting an interview. The first is to take notes on everything the subject says. The second is to commit everything to memory and then write it or type it as soon as possible (before you get it all mixed up). The third method is to use a tape recorder.

The trouble with note taking is that it can be distracting to the interviewee. He is constantly being made aware that his every word is being written down for possible later use. Not only that, you will find it difficult if not impossible to jot everything down and at the same time formulate additional questions as you do.

As for committing material to memory, it can cost you a great story if you don't remember all the details in the exact order they were mentioned. And you can leave yourself open for a libel suit if you garble things. Even if you report everything without a mistake, you have no proof that what you wrote is what the subject said.

Using a tape recorder is definitely the way to go. Advise your subject at the start that you will be recording him so there is no misunderstanding later. Use a modern compact recorder with a built-in microphone, and within a minute or two your subject will forget completely that he is being recorded and be much more open with you.

Transcribe your own tape interviews rather than hiring someone to do it for you, at least in the beginning. By transcribing the tape yourself, you will automatically sort out the good responses from the bad and at the same time give your article its own unique form and continuity. You will also find that your writing skills are being honed in the process.

In the course of going over the tape, you will undoubtedly pick up points that you hadn't even noticed during the actual interview. Also, by transcribing yourself, you can be sure you get every single word correctly in quoting your source.

By the way, you may be surprised to discover that even well-educated people don't speak the king's English. You find people using split infinitives, mixing singular nouns and plural verbs, and speaking in incomplete sentences. So how do you quote them without making them appear like illiterates? The rule is that you should correct their grammar and even transpose words when necessary, as long as you don't change the meaning of what they are saying.

You may also discover during the transcription process that you have enough material for two or three different articles, rather than just a single one.

WHOM TO INTERVIEW. You can find interesting people everywhere. And they will usually agree to an interview. The trick is then to find a market for the material you gather. It's a case of which comes first, the chicken or the egg. Some writers interview people and search for a magazine where their article will fit. Others pick a magazine and then search for people to interview whose story will fit the publication. With rare exception, we advise the former—finding interesting people and *then* seeking a market for the interview article.

Some elitists may claim that the world is full of boobs, few of whom have anything intelligent to say about anything.

We have found the opposite to be true. Take a close look and you can find interesting people and great stories all around you. Start with your own friends and your friends' friends. If you have an "inside line" to someone, you will have a much easier time arranging an interview than by dealing with total strangers, going through press agents, and the like.

Take a close look at the people with whom you work, those who live in your neighborhood, those you went to school with, even people you've met on vacations. You may discover that the fellow who runs the corner grocery store was a World War II flying ace who faced danger and death on a daily basis. Or the paper boy may be a Golden Gloves hopeful, with dreams of one day becoming another Muhammed Ali. Maybe the mailman is building a fifty-foot sailboat in his backyard and someday plans to sail off into the sunset.

The stories are there. All you have to do is go out and find them. And you will find that the more unlikely the subject of the interview, the easier it is to sell the article.

WHAT TO ASK. Getting people to open up is an art. It comes with experience and intelligent preparation. But it can be learned.

1. Starting an interview isn't difficult. Tell the person that you are interested in his work or activities and you'd like to learn more. This approach is a good icebreaker. If the inter-

viewee makes small talk, let him—it will help to loosen him up.

2. Next, ask about how the person got his idea, break, or start—how it happened, what happened.

If the person just won't open up, it could be because he is simply shy. Or, especially in the case of celebrities, he may have been burned in another interview. In either case, it is up to you to win the person's confidence and set him at ease. Show him that you are interested in him as a person and that his story will be of interest to countless others. (It's called the old ego inflater ploy.)

3. If your subject becomes argumentative and belligerent, shift the emphasis and ask him to comment on something else.

4. If your subject begins talking "over your head," explain that you are just a layman, as are the readers of the magazine, and you would like him to put things in a way that everyone can comprehend.

5. Never allow your own opinions to work their way into the interview. Suppose, for example, that you are talking to a toy manufacturer whose products are distasteful or senseless in your mind. Rather than simply stating this, ask the executive if he feels children's toys are becoming more related to violence than toys of the 1950s. You have thus broached a delicate subject without personally offending your interviewee.

6. If your subject responds to your questions with boring answers, he may simply be a boring person, in which case you laid an egg in picking him as the subject of an article. On the other hand, it could be that you just aren't asking good questions.

7. If you make a faux pas during the interview, don't try to weasel out of it. Admit your mistake. Likewise, if you misquote someone and are corrected, don't let it throw you.

8. Don't bluff about matters that you really don't fully understand. You are there to ask questions and to learn something, not to impress the interviewee with your knowl-

edge. Let your ignorance of a subject be an asset by asking questions that most others would also ask.

When a person grants you an interview, it means that he is letting you enter his sanctuary. Your job is to gather information while avoiding the urge to editorialize. Let your subject do that for himself. People are interested in what he has to say, not what you have to say about what he has to say.

The First-Person Article

Over the years, the myth has been perpetuated that writing in the first person ("I") is an amateurish way of approaching a story. Perhaps it is because whenever youngsters are asked to produce an essay for their English class, it winds up as a first-person account of some event in their lives.

But the use of the first person for articles can be most effective, especially when you find yourself in a situation or a chain of events that is way out of the ordinary. In such a case first-person usage helps your readers to put themselves in your shoes and vicariously go through the experience with you.

For example, suppose you wangled an interview with a famous movie star, and instead of proceeding with the standard interview, your subject enticed you into spending a wild night "on the town." What better way to provide a glimpse into the "real" Mr. or Ms. So-and-so then through a first-person account of the episode. And don't worry about violating the person's privacy. The person in question was aware that you are a writer and were seeing him for the express purpose of getting a story. If he didn't want the publicity, he shouldn't have taken you along on his jaunt.

A different kind of example that illustrates when first-person narrative works best involves a ski trip we once took to the remote reaches of western Canada. We were on assignment for a ski magazine to do an article on helicopter skiing in the infamous Cariboo Mountains.

Our original plan was to zero in on the kind of people who

go on such an adventure rather than spend two weeks in a posh resort such as Aspen or Vail. But in the course of our visit, we found ourselves stalked by timber wolves, dropped on nameless mountain peaks fifty miles from the nearest road, and almost buried alive in an avalanche. There was only one way to capture the real feeling of a trip like this—in the first person.

Another excellent example of when to use the first-person approach is when you are digging out a story "incognito." Suppose you take a job as an aide in a mental institution to see what kind of treatment the inmates really get. Or suppose you hire on as a waiter to see how it feels to deal with people in a service-related occupation. Obviously, the first-person approach is called for in such instances.

Third-Person Narrative

Third-person narrative is the technique used by most fiction writers in novels and short stories. It places you as reader in a spectator role, much like the audience of a play.

Can it work for nonfiction magazine articles? Most definitely yes. The way you do it is to approach a subject as if you are going to write a short story about it, complete with character development, plot, and climax. Unless you have these makings, you are better off to go with a straight "report the facts" approach.

Among the masters of the third-person narrative are writers such as Truman Capote (*In Cold Blood* is the ultimate example of applying narrative technique to nonfiction material) and Norman Mailer.

All of which brings us around to a discussion of the most recent development in nonfiction writing—the so-called New Journalism.

The "New Journalism"

The "new journalists" came into prominence in the 1960s,

and many still employ this approach to reporting today. In short, the "new journalists" have simply adapted a variety of literary devices formerly limited in use to the writing of fiction and applied them to reporting of news and features for newspapers and magazines.

The "new journalists" see themselves as a new wave, but in fact their idea is far from original. Former journalists turned authors from Mark Twain to Ernest Hemingway employed fiction-writing techniques in their news writing to great effect.

In general, though, the "new journalism" method of writing really lends itself much more to magazine writing than to newspaper reporting. That is because the use of fiction-writing techniques precludes the possibility of keeping the article short (or at least under several thousand words).

Who are the "new journalists"? They include the likes of George Plimpton, Tom Wolfe, Gay Talese, Truman Capote, Norman Mailer, and Terry Southern.

As a free-lance magazine article writer, you should read the work of these new journalists to determine whether their techniques will work (at least occasionally) for you, too. Generally, you will find that the types of publications that lean toward this method of writing are the so-called alternative publications—the *Village Voice, Rolling Stone,* and others of this genre.

This is important to remember, because if you were to produce a piece written as a short story and filled with devices such as stream of consciousness, you would not be apt to sell the article to the *Ladies' Home Journal* or *Boys' Life* magazine.

Borrowing Newspaper Techniques

Just because you are writing an article for a magazine, don't hesitate to borrow tricks of the newspaper business in producing your story.

The "grabber" headline is a good example. Put a title on

your story that really makes the editor want to read it, and chances are he will. Not only that, he'll probably use your headline idea when he lays the article out in the magazine.

Another standard newspaper device is to put "punch" into the lead paragraph. Granted, you have a good deal of latitude in writing your magazine article, but starting it with a blockbuster of a statement is a surefire way to keep the reader's attention—especially if your article deals with something that is exclusive or sensational.

Finally, don't hesitate to use the newspaper reporter's technique of summing up at the end of your article, especially if it is a "how-to" type piece.

Writing Fiction for Magazines

So far, we have pretty much been discussing the writing of nonfiction pieces for magazines. But many magazines also buy fiction of various types, from the short story to the novelette to the complete novel (which is usually serialized).

Fiction appears regularly in men's magazines such as *Playboy*, *Esquire*, and *Penthouse*. It appears in women's magazines such as *Redbook* and *Cosmopolitan*. And it appears in sports and other special interest magazines, too.

Generally speaking, fiction authors aim their material at books rather than magazines. When they sell a piece to a magazine, it is either to help promote book sales or to provide a little needed revenue to "tide them over" a rough spot.

Most free-lance magazine article writers stick to nonfiction because this is where the greatest market is, and this is generally easier to write than fiction. We're not trying to dissuade you from cranking out fiction pieces for sale to magazines. (The "true love" and sex magazines eat up fiction pieces.) But you should be aware that it generally takes a good deal longer to produce a salable fiction piece than a nonfiction article, but both articles generally earn the same level of payment, all other factors being equal.

Another problem with writing fiction for magazines is that most have their "pet" fiction writers and pretty much stick to them. Breaking into this area of the writing marketplace is a good deal tougher than going the nonfiction route.

The Travel Article

While the travel article can be written in any number of ways, it also deserves a special classification as a particular genre of article. In recent years, especially, travel articles have been in strong demand, thanks in part to beefed-up travel and vacation sections in metropolitan newspapers, and thanks to the arrival on the scene of a number of specialty travel magazines—*Town & Country, Holiday, Travel and Leisure,* the various in-flight magazines, to name just a few.

Travel articles have wide appeal. First, they help the person who actually does a good deal of traveling, either for pleasure or business. Second, they offer a vicarious pleasure to the armchair traveler, who will probably never get to visit the places he reads about.

Regardless of the approach taken by the writer, the travel article has to provide certain vital information to do its job well. It's not enough to paint an elaborate picture of a particular vacation spot or destination. The reader also needs to know travel costs (including comparisons of popular package prices), the best time to go, the best way to get there, recommended dining and shopping spots, what currency is needed, and similar information.

Unless you are writing a roundup of many vacation spots, don't fall into the trap of generalizing. Rather than attempting to discuss a coast-to-coast motor-home trip in a single article, zero in instead on a single region, such as the Colorado Rockies. You'll be able to provide much more salient facts, and the reader won't feel overwhelmed.

Another tip for new travel writers—don't just paint a rosy picture of the place in question. If there are bad points, you owe it to your reader to mention them. Nothing could be worse than for some poor soul to conjure up visions of paradise from reading your glowing report, only to discover the place is overrun with mosquitoes and hotter than heck.

The great thing about travel writing is that magazines never seem to get too much information on a particular place. With costs going up and down periodically, and with new hotels and attractions going in at major destination resorts, no place gets too much publicity. *Holiday* may have run an article about Paris a year ago, but a fresh piece will still appeal to its readers.

The clincher for travel writers is that to do the story right, you have to visit the place. Fortunately, many airlines, hotels, chambers of commerce, and national tourist offices go out of their way to accommodate travel writers. And once you begin to make a name for yourself, you'll find you seldom have to pay for travel, accommodations, meals, or sightseeing. *And* you'll be given the red carpet treatment in most places.

The Humor Market

Writing humorous articles may come easily for some, but for most writers it is the most difficult assignment of all. You either have this special talent, or you don't. The danger in writing a humorous piece is not that it will turn out to be not funny but that it will be corny or, worse, sticky sweet and sentimental.

Writing for Kids

A lot of newcomers to the free-lance writing game assume that writing for children's publications is easy—or at least easier than writing for adults. Wrong! Just because you used to be a child, or because you have a pack of kids running around the house, it doesn't mean that you will be able to see things in a way that appeals to a child.

Writing for kids is like walking a tightrope—it is a strict discipline. On the one hand, you can't use language that youngsters just don't comprehend. On the other hand, if you "talk down" to your young readers, they'll sense it immediately. Children look for facts and information in articles, just as adults do, but they need them on their own level.

But don't patronize your readers either. Using "hip" terms and slang will get you into more trouble than it will get you out of. What is "in" today may be "out" by the time your article reaches the reader.

Perhaps the best way to get a feel for what kids read is to purchase a number of children's magazines and books and scrutinize them closely. You will discover that each age group requires its own special kind of writing. Like we said, writing for kids isn't easy!

Writing for Business

Articles about business can be divided into two distinct types. The first is the article that is written for the layman, or average guy. Your job is to take complicated business information and "decode" it for popular consumption.

The second type of business article is one that is written for the "in crowd," or people in the business community. In this case your mission is not to simplify basic concepts but to provide the kind of facts and information that the working businessman will find valuable in the operation of his business, in the buying and selling of stocks, bonds, and commodities, or in mapping plans for the future.

The business writer, just like the sports writer, has a good deal more latitude than other writers in interjecting opinion with facts. Many business writers are regarded as authorities in particular fields (such as Elliott Janeway for stocks and bonds), and businessmen look to you for advice and predictions of future developments.

Obviously you will have a leg up on the competition if your background includes a major in business, accounting, economics, or a related field in college. And if you have worked in the business world for a period of time, so much the better.

What is vitally important is that you are able to find your way around in the world of business and that you know (or learn quickly) where to go for specific information. To be accepted by other businessmen, you have to fit in with their life-style.

Long hair and blue jeans just won't cut it on Wall Street or in an ad agency on Chicago's Michigan Avenue. You've got to dress, look, and act the part. That means suit and tie, attache case, and appropriate credit cards, among other things.

If business writing is to be your primary pursuit, then you should make a point of being as informed as possible at all times. That means reading the *Wall Street Journal, Forbes Magazine, Business Week, Time, Newsweek,* the *New York Times, Crain's Chicago Business,* and as many other such publications as you can obtain.

Not only will these publications keep you abreast of developments in all areas of business but you will find inumerable story leads in your daily perusal of the business pages.

In approaching executives for information, don't assume that you will have a difficult time. Businessmen have big egos, and the higher up the corporate ladder you go in your research, the bigger the egos tend to be. So when the president or chairman of the board learns that you, a business writer, wish to interview him, he'll do his darndest to find time for you.

Pick a Base of Operation

Some of the more successful business writers have established themselves not so much as authorities on a particular field, such as steel manufacturing or oil drilling, but rather as competent generalists who know a specific geographical region and have many contacts there.

Suppose, for example, that you decide to make Chicago your home base. You routinely find stories here and file them with various business magazines. *Forbes* decides that it wants to do a report on the growing mail order sales market. Since both Sears, Roebuck and Montgomery Ward are headquartered in the Chicago area, you are given the assignment.

Naturally, if you intend to earn a living as a free-lance business writer, you have to locate in one of the nation's major business centers—preferably New York, Chicago, Houston, or Los Angeles. Not only will these centers generate enough business article possibilities to keep you busy on a full-time basis but they are situated so that should something develop in a nearby "secondary" center, you can cover it on your own or on assignment from a magazine.

For example, from New York you are in easy striking distance of such cities as Philadelphia, Boston, Baltimore, and Washington, D.C. From Chicago you are close to Milwaukee, Saint Louis, Minneapolis, and Detroit. From Los Angeles you can reach San Diego, San Francisco, Las Vegas, and even such cities as Portland and Seattle much easier than can someone coming from a magazine's home office somewhere east of the Rockies.

One of the nice things about business writing is that you can be wrong 50 percent of the time and no one will raise an eyebrow. The stock market watchers are perfect proof of this. When they miss the boat by a country mile, they just chalk it off to some "whim" of the buyers or sellers.

Science Writing

No field has a greater need for well-written, clearly understood articles than the broad spectrum of science. Thanks to the explosion in the computer field, plus rapid advancement in most other areas from aerospace to pharmaceuticals, there is much more to write about than there are people to do the writing.

But if you intend to try your hand at producing scientifically oriented articles, you had better be sure you understand your subject thoroughly. In no other area of magazine writing can you fall on your face so quickly.

Other Specialized Fields

If you feel that specializing in a particular field will pay off in the long run, there are certainly a vast number of subjects to zero in on. Among others that offer the greatest possibilities for producing salable articles on a regular basis are agriculture, sports, politics, and religion.

What about hot areas such as the women's movement? They are great for the short run, but many such categories fizzle out over the long haul, at least in terms of story possibilities. Then you will be faced with starting all over in a different area.

Summing It Up

No matter what kind of article or articles you elect to write, you must always keep in mind exactly whom you are writing for and guide your efforts in that direction. Likewise, limit your article to one idea. If you have ten closely related ideas, write ten separate articles rather than trying to squeeze them all into a single one. Finally, remember that research is the key to good articles.

5

Photojournalism

Photojournalists are a relatively new breed of cat, having evolved since the time of World War II, when correspondents began carrying cameras out of necessity. The rise of magazines such as *Life* and *Look* provided the perfect avenue for photo stories, and the term photojournalist was born.

The photojournalist is essentially a writer who carries a camera, as opposed to a photographer who also happens to write. In our years as journalists we've known scores of reporters and writers who carried cameras but no photographers who went the other way.

Perhaps the reason is that while both writing and photography can legitimately be labeled as art forms, photography is also a science and as such can be mastered by anyone with a working knowledge of elementary physics, chemistry, and mathematics, whereas creative writing is a much more nebulous undertaking.

Yes, you can "write by the numbers," so to speak—at least you can produce routine news stories with the "who, what, where, when, and why" formula. But producing anything more complex, including magazine articles, requires that certain magical ingredient called creativity.

Now, before we get all the photographers up in arms, we have to backtrack and point out that "lining them up and shooting them," as most occasional photographers do, is a far cry from what real pros do. When most photojournalists come up with the prizewinning photo, it is usually by accident rather than design.

Magazines have led the way in the field of photojournalism, partly because most newspapers are tradition-bound and refuse to accept the fact that a person can both report and take photos on assignment. Then, too, the American Newspaper Guild has been charged with opposing the creation of photojournalist slots in editorial departments of many papers in the belief that the designation is really just another way for management to reduce the number of editorial staffers.

Most magazines, even those with large editorial staffs, use free-lancers for much of their material. One reason is that even regional magazines must cover a good deal more territory than even the largest newspapers, so free-lancers are a real necessity.

So, doesn't it make sense for an editor to send a single photojournalist rather than a writer and a photographer on assignment whenever possible? The savings in expenses (which many magazines pay free-lancers) is considerable, even for a single assignment. Over the course of a year the difference could spell the difference between a loss and a healthy profit, especially for smaller magazines.

As far as the photojournalist is concerned, he is able to earn more money for a given story because he is being paid for both his writing and his photos. But that also means he'll be hustling a lot more than when he was just doing the writing. It also means that there is less margin for error, because if he goofs, he'll be so busy that there is little chance for backtracking and correcting a mistake.

Should you make the switch and go from "just plain writer" to photojournalist? We say yes, for the following reasons:

1. You will get more free-lance assignments from magazines of all types.
2. You will have a much better chance of selling articles you do "on speculation."
3. You will earn a good deal more money per time spent on articles.
4. Doing double duty as writer/photographer will force you to improve your reporting ability.
5. Photography is fun!

Necessary Gear

The immediate reaction of most free-lance writers is that they couldn't possibly become a photojournalist because of the expense involved. They look at their associates who are professional photographers and shudder at the sight of all that expensive (and heavy) gear most of them tote around.

Take heart. You really need just a few basic photographic tools to do a good job in 99 percent of the stories you go after. The reason some professional photographers carry so much stuff is that (a) they lack confidence and fall back on the extra gear as a crutch, and (b) camera gear is a status symbol to amateurs and pros alike—the more they carry, the better a photographer they are (at least, that's what the rest of us are supposed to think).

So what do you really need? Here are our suggestions for all you erstwhile photojournalists:

1. Two of the new ultra lightweight 35-mm single-lens camera bodies (preferably with automatic exposure capability).

We think the Olympus OM-2 is the obvious choice because (a) it is one of the smallest, lightest cameras around, (b) it is sturdy and dependable, and (c) it can be repaired just about anywhere your work takes you.
  2. The following lenses:

    28-mm wide-angle
    100-mm telephoto
    200-mm telephoto
    35/85-mm zoom

  3. The following filters:

    ultraviolet
    skylight
    yellow or red

  4. A powerful, battery-operated electronic flash unit, which has the capability of taking long-distance night shots and providing "bounce flash" lighting.
  5. A "fanny" pack for toting extra lenses, camera bodies, film packs, etc. on assignment.

Why two camera bodies? Because there will be times when you want to take black-and-white *and* color photos for the same article. Load one camera with B&W film and the other with color slides, and you will be ready for any eventuality.

Why so many lenses? Well, the wide-angle (28-mm) lets you shoot crowds in tight quarters, as well as panoramic nature scenes. The 100-mm telephoto lens is perfect for portrait shots as well as most sporting events, the 200-mm for events where you just can't get in close (such as yacht races, auto races, and horse races), and the 35/85 zoom lens for the ability to go from wide angle to short telephoto in a second or two.

When you carry two camera bodies, you not only have B&W and color capability, you also have two different lenses available for both films. Switching bayonet-mount lenses such as those found on Olympus cameras takes just a flick of the wrist.

As for the filters, they aren't a necessity, but they will improve your photos: the ultraviolet will cut out glare and unwanted reflections; the yellow or red filter will provide dramatic contrast between clouds and sky for B&W films; and the skylight filter will help reduce the bluish cast that can be seen on some days in the distance as well as protect the surface of the lenses from being scratched.

The "fanny" pack is another nonnecessity that can be a real blessing, especially when your article requires you to do a lot of walking and writing at the same time. The pack leaves your hands free.

How to Develop Skills

As with any other pursuit, you can read the instruction book and then just go out and learn by doing. But if you ask anyone who has taught himself to golf, or ski, or play tennis, they'll tell you they wish they would have taken lessons at the beginning.

For one thing, you'll learn the skill much, much more quickly. And you'll avoid developing bad habits that you'll just have to break later.

In most large metropolitan centers you can find a number of photography courses available—some at high schools and colleges, some at YMCAs, libraries, and the like, and some at privately operated studios. Many of these privately operated studios also have all necessary equipment for processing film and making slides and prints. In some cases you can rent the equipment and space for an hourly fee. In other cases you will be required to join a photo club or group in order to use the gear.

Even if you live in a small town, away from the madding

crowds, you can learn to be a pretty fair photographer by taking a correspondence course. (Check the various photography magazines for ads.)

Of course, learning how to use a camera and developing the knack for spotting the right shots to enhance your article are two different things. The second comes only from practice and plenty of film. And remember that film is cheap. The best photographers for magazines go through film by the yardful. Their philosophy is that if you shoot a hundred pictures and use five the cost is just a few dollars, but if you shoot five and don't sell any, you just lost out on several hundred dollars in sales.

Here are a few more tips as you launch your photojournalistic career:

- Always send 8 x 10 black-and-white glossies rather than proof sheets with your articles. The editor will be able to really see what you're selling, and your chances of having him use more than one picture will be improved.
- Never send original color slides. It costs just pennies to have copies made.
- Send slides in clear plastic cases to protect them from getting scratched.
- Always send stamped, addressed envelopes if you want your photos returned.
- If the magazine insists on buying first *and* all other rights to your photos, *double* the price. Remember, you won't be able to realize any additional revenue once you sell all rights.

part III
Selling Your Articles

6

Making Contact

It doesn't do any good to invest days or even weeks of your time producing an article if no one is interested in buying it. So how do you know if your idea has any value before you begin the laborious task of researching and writing your story? You send out query letters to magazine editors, describing the idea you have and briefly explaining why you believe it would be a good article for this or that magazine.

Your idea may be terrific, but if it doesn't fit into a particular magazine's editorial plans, you might as well forget it—unless you are writing for your own pleasure, that is.

If an editor likes your idea, he'll respond, either with a note or a phone call, advising you what he wants in terms of article length, photos, and collateral materials (charts, graphs, or illustrations). He'll also advise you as to what he's willing to pay and what his deadline requirements are.

Keep in mind that even though you get a green light, the

editor is not under any mandate to use your article. If he decides he doesn't like it—for any reason—upon receipt, he can simply send it back.

It is his responsibility to return any rejected manuscripts promptly so that you can have the best chance of selling your article somewhere else. You have the responsibility of meeting all deadlines that are spelled out to you. Failure to get your stuff in on time is a sure way to get it back with a rejection slip.

Editors read scores of manuscripts each week, some sent in on assignment, some sent in like yours as a result of a query, and some simply sent in "cold"—in other words, on speculation. This means the competition among free-lance writers can be fierce, at least on the major magazines. (That's why as a newcomer to the free-lance ranks, you really should aim for smaller regional and specialty magazines, at least until you make a name for yourself.)

Here's something else to think about. No matter how good your article is, if it isn't presented properly, it will be rejected. It should be professionally done—double spaced, with page numbers placed properly, and accompanied by a cover letter. If it comes across the editor's desk looking like the product of a high school dropout—typographical errors, scratched-out words, arrows, smudges and wrinkles—the editor will automatically assume this is a second-rate piece.

When an editor accepts an article idea on speculation, it means just that—he is speculating that your idea is a good one and he wants to see more. And you as the writer are speculating that you can produce a top-notch article, superior even to what his own staff can do. He wants a piece that he can't get anywhere else, with an angle that only you can provide. Magazines don't pay top dollars for stories that are marginal.

Once you've sent in your query and the editor has responded positively, you can then submit your feature. There are no second chances, so the article had better be good. You aren't going to get a reply that says that the ending is weak, or page two is confusing. If the editor doesn't like your piece in its entirety, he will simply reject it.

If you regularly submit articles to the same magazines and they are continually rejected, you'll eventually get a reputation as "some kind of a nut," and then your stuff won't even get a glance before it is returned. Even if you finally stumble across the story of the decade, no one will know because no one will ever see it, except a secretary, that is.

Dealing with Editors

Editors are a different breed of cat. Virtually every one got his start as a cub reporter on a paper or obscure magazine somewhere and then worked his way "up the ladder," to copy editor, then copy desk chief, then managing editor (or executive editor, or simply editor).

Generally, editors were pretty fair writers, but few were outstanding. Most outstanding writers stay writers—it's in the blood. Nonetheless, most editors secretly feel that if they really set their minds to it, they could produce better articles than most that cross their desks.

In other words, editors can be very picky indeed. And since your only contact will be your query letter, it will be a direct reflection on you. Obviously, the query is an important document.

How to Write a Query Letter

Your query is essentially no different from any other business letter. To be most effective, it should be brief and to the point. Editors, like other busy executives, have neither the time nor the inclination to wade through a lot of tinsel in an effort to determine your point.

You can save a lot of letter-writing time by checking in the Ayer directory or in the *Writer's Market* book to determine the type of material various magazines are interested in before composing your query letter.

If you've got an idea for an article on white-water canoeing on Wisconsin's Wolf River, you've got a much better chance of selling it to outdoor-oriented magazines such as *Mariah* and *Outside* than you do to a magazine such as *Sports Illustrated* or *Colorado*.

Generally your query should be no more than a page in length. Usually this is sufficient to get a reply one way or the other. Occasionally, an editor will write back and ask for an outline, especially if your article will be lengthy or complex in nature.

If you have an idea for a headline, or title, for your article, mention it in your letter. And if you have some ideas for a special layout, mention that, too. Even if the editor doesn't take your advice or suggestion, he is now aware that you have given more than a passing thought to how the article will fit into his publication.

It won't hurt to tell the editor why you believe your article will be of special interest to his readers and why it is different from others of its type. Editors may be smart, but they can't read minds. You have to spell out your ideas.

Indicate the estimated length of the article, and state whether you have photos or other illustrations to go with your article.

Here is a sample query:

> Dear Mr. Smith:
> While the city of Montreal has some of the coldest winters of any major city, Canadians have found a way to avoid the freezing temperatures and snow.
> They have built an underground city within their city, complete with shops, walkways, and other attractions, all temperature regulated and climate controlled. Visitors can attend a symphony concert or ballet performance, followed by dinner and drinks at an intimate bistro, and never once have to don their overcoats.

I have recently returned from a visit to this underground metropolis and can provide a feature article tailored to your needs, as well as 8 x 10 black-and-white glossy photos.

Please advise if you'd like to receive such an article on speculation, and please specify the length you prefer.

Sincerely,

John Jones
234 Fifth St.
New York, N.Y. 10117
Phone: 212-555-2222

If the editor likes your idea, he is apt to respond with a note like this:

Dear Mr. Jones:
Your suggestion for a piece on Montreal's underground city sounds interesting.

We'd like the opportunity to see it. Can you sent us 2,000 words plus five or six B&W photos by May 5? We seldom use color pictures, but if you have any exceptional ones, we'd like to take a look at them on the outside chance that we could use one.

FYI, we pay five cents a word, plus $20 for each B&W photo used and $50 for color shots.

Sincerely,

John Doe
Editor
Vacation Magazine

Your next step is not to write the article but to send off a brief note, acknowledging receipt of the editor's letter and advising him that you will comply with his request. Why all this writing back and forth? Because it is a courtesy on your part to let the editor know that you will be proceeding with an article according to his requirements.

Remember, he is dealing with as many as twenty-five or thirty writers at a time, and he keeps a "budget" or schedule of articles for various issues. Being advised that your article is definitely in the works makes the editor's job just a bit easier, and chances are that when you send a query for another article in the future, he'll be even more receptive because of your professionalism.

When you send in your completed manuscript, be sure it is accompanied by a cover letter in which you restate the fact that you are submitting the article on speculation, based on the letter from the editor. (Don't forget he is deluged with correspondence and manuscripts daily, so a gentle reminder that this is one he asked for will help jog his memory.)

Suppose you send in the article and you don't hear from the editor for several weeks or more? Don't panic. In the case of manuscripts sent to magazines, no news is almost always good news. It means that your article has been accepted and is "in the works."

Keep in mind that most magazines operate on deadlines that are as far as six months or more in advance of the publication date. And since most magazines pay for articles upon publication, there will be a definite time lag between acceptance and payment.

This puts you as a free-lance writer in roughly the same position as the small businessman, where accounts receivable almost always lag behind sales. In short, you are apt to face a cash flow problem for the first year or so, until payments equal accepted stories.

If the suspense is killing you, and you just can't wait several months to learn if your article really was accepted, you can always send a short note to inquire. But avoid using the phone unless you have become a fairly regular contributor to the magazine in question and have established some kind of rapport with the staff. Calling "cold" can rankle an editor, especially if he's right on deadline and has fifteen things to take care of when the phone rings.

No one, including editors, likes to be patronized, but that doesn't mean you shouldn't show respect for his position by following commonly accepted practices as a writer.

Packaging Your Product

Ask people who market everything from soapflakes to kids' cereals how they feel about packaging, and they'll tell you it is at least as important in selling a product as the quality of the product itself.

Obviously this isn't true of magazine articles, but packaging certainly is important. If your materials arrive looking as if they were professionally prepared, your chances of selling the contents are enhanced.

Earlier we stated some basics to remember, such as double spacing and keeping your work neat looking. When you send it, your package should also be neat. Send your manuscript in a large envelope so that it can be shipped flat with any photos. And insert several pieces of cardboard to provide stiffness and keep the photos from being bent while in the custody of the U.S. Postal Service.

Finally, don't forget to enclose a stamped, addressed envelope, so that the materials can be returned should they be rejected. (Editors are not obligated to return materials not accompanied by a stamped envelope.)

7

Legal Matters

As a free-lance writer you have a number of legal matters to deal with on a regular basis. Some deal with the content of your articles—avoiding libel, slander, invasion of privacy, and misappropriation, and protection of your work by copyright. The other important legal area of concern for you will be the business of taxes on the money you earn.

Libel

Your writing can be construed as libelous if it tends to expose another individual to public hatred, contempt, or ridicule. It matters not whether your statements are true or false. The determining factor in libel suits is the result on another individual.

The easiest way to avoid the possibility of a libel suit against you and/or the magazine that publishes your article is simply to avoid any statements that could be harmful to another person. Of course, if your article is of a sensational nature, taking all such references out may also remove the very guts of the article. So the final decision is yours—and the editor's.

Some people are excluded from the protection of the laws of libel. These include politicians, movie and TV stars, and various other celebrities and well-known individuals who are classified as "public figures."

The only way such public figures can win a libel suit is to prove "actual malice" by the publication of false defamatory material with knowledge that it was false or with reckless disregard of whether it was false or not. At least this is how the U.S. Supreme Court has interpreted the law.

The justices also decreed that there must be proof that the information was published with a high degree of awareness of probable falsity, and sufficient evidence must also exist that the writer and/or publisher had serious doubts as to the truth of the article.

It doesn't take a degree in jurisprudence to see that the law is weighted heavily in favor of the writer, at least in regard to public figures.

When you are dealing with potentially dangerous editorial copy about other individuals, play it safe, and have the magazine you submit the article to get clearance from its own attorney before publishing it.

Invasion of Privacy

The arrival of the electronic age brought with it inherent problems regarding the protection of the privacy of individuals. Early telephones, for example, had as many as a dozen different people using the same "party line," so the caller was always a little cautious about saying anything that could get him into hot water.

The advent of the private line seemed to solve the problem,

but it didn't take long for electronics wizards to create tiny listening devices, or "bugs," for eavesdropping on private conversations. When that was thwarted, they could always resort to wiretapping somewhere along the line or even in the telephone terminal.

Then came television, and soon this ingenious device was turned into a method for spying on people. Walk into a large department store, or bank, or even a high-rise apartment building, and you are apt to see a tiny TV camera scanning the area. On the other side is a guard or attendant whose job it is to keep his eye on you!

It's not hard to understand how our society has become more than a little paranoid about Big Brother watching every move. As a result, the courts have been leaning more and more in favor of protecting the privacy of an individual in every way possible. (And don't get us wrong—we're in favor of protecting the privacy of individuals, even when it makes our job as writer more difficult.)

How do recent court rulings affect you in your pursuit of story material? Individuals are protected in the following ways:

1. From appropriation of their names or likeness for advertising purposes or purposes of trade.

Take the recent case where a dead ringer of a football star Joe Namath endorsed a particular product. The court ruled that Joe was entitled to remuneration as well as future protection, since he didn't give his permission.

2. From intrusion, where the writer "butts in" where he could not reasonably be expected.

Suppose, for example, that you crashed a private party and while there uncovered some embarrassing or damaging information about one of the parties. Using such material could lead to a suit against you, and the odds are stacked against you.

3. Public revelation of private facts that are embarrassing, regardless of their truthfulness.

An example of this is the case where a man in the crowd during an appearance by then President Gerald Ford spotted another man pull a gun out and point it at the chief executive. The first man wrestled the gun away from the other man and was hailed as a hero.

But subsequent investigation by reporters revealed that the hero was a homosexual, and that information was plastered across the front pages of several publications. The man sued and won, and rightly so.

4. Being put in a false light in the public eye.

Some writers shrug their shoulders at the mention of the dangers when writing sensational material about individuals. Granted, it is a fact that the vast majority of people who are the subjects of such articles never bother to take the matter to court.

They assume they don't have a chance of winning, and even if they were to win, the case could be drawn out for years, at great expense to themselves. Not only that, the legal action would simply keep the matter in the public eye for that much longer. Far better, they reason, to simply let the matter die.

But suppose you take the cavalier attitude of many writers and simply disregard problems dealing with privacy laws. Even if just one person out of a hundred pursues the matter in court, you'll suffer, too, regardless of the outcome of the case.

More than one writer and publication have been literally bankrupted (even with liability insurance) as a result of a drawn-out court case.

If you want to be a smart writer, observe this simple rule: "When in doubt, leave it out."

There is another side to the coin—some legal experts believe the tougher application of privacy laws will result in a thwarting of the freedom of the press, itself guaranteed by our Constitution.

In a recent article in *Editor & Publisher* (the trade journal for the newspaper fraternity), Harvard Law School professor

Dr. Arthur Miller cited these three points as examples of unwarranted use of privacy restrictions:

1. Reverse freedom of information suits, as in the case of a hospital's going to court to prevent a reporter from obtaining Medicare reports for an article on spiraling hospital costs.

2. The prevention of personal finance disclosure by political candidates and officeholders.

3. Bans on the use of tape recorders by reporters.

The dilemma is that of the rights of individuals clashing with the rights of freedom of the press (included in the Bill of Rights to protect those very individuals). Judges find themselves "damned if they do and damned if they don't" rule one way or the other.

The only real solution is for voluntary restraint by all sides.

Copyright Law

As a free-lance writer you have to think about protecting the article you write from misappropriation by others, or else you will be putting in a good deal of work so that others can benefit financially.

The copyright protects your ownership of a manuscript in the same way that a patent protects the invention of an individual. In most cases, magazines copyright everything that appears in each issue as a routine practice. And that means your material is protected.

An obvious problem is just who owns the article once it appears in print? The answer is that unless you sign over all rights to the article, it is your property, even though the magazine has paid you for its use.

That means you can later sell it to another publication, or you can take material from it for use in other articles. You also have the right to make reprints of the article for promotional purposes, although if you use the name of the magazine, you must obtain permission.

Should you file for your own copyright, even though the magazine in which it appears is copyrighted? The answer is yes, especially if the contents of your article are spectacular.

To copyright an article, include the required copyright notice (the symbol © and the word "Copyright") plus the year of publication and the names of the copyright proprietor (your byline) on all copies. Then file a claim to copyright along with a $6 fee and two copies of the article.

A copyright is good for the life of the author plus an additional fifty years. That means that if you ever do write something that becomes a classic, your heirs will be able to cash in well into the twenty-first century.

One surprising aspect to the copyright laws is that there really is not any time limit for filing. The law states you must file "promptly," but there have been cases where writers and publishers waited as long as twenty-seven years before filing, and the courts ruled it was still legal.

The only hitch for those who see this as a loophole for avoiding those $6 fees is that should you file after the time of publication, you could be subject to a fine from the Register of Copyrights. Another hitch is that if you discover that another magazine has pirated your article, or parts of it, you can't start a law suit until *after* you file for a copyright.

In any case, you can rest easy, because you are covered from the time your article first appears in print.

Taxes and the Writer

Next to waiters and waitresses, the most badgered group of individuals when it comes to payment of income taxes is writers of all kinds, be they playrights, poets, or free-lance magazine writers such as you.

The reason is that it is fairly easy for writers and waiters to avoid declaring all of their income, so Uncle Sam figures that by putting on the pressure, he can intimidate you into paying "your fair share."

Legal Matters 69

Sure, some writers do set out to "screw the system," as it were. But the vast majority of us are just like most other people—we don't even think about cheating on our taxes. Unfortunately, most writers share a common fault—they are totally careless, sloppy, and inept when it comes to maintaining decent records of their income and expenses.

In fact, most writers can't even tell you how well they are doing on a day-to-day basis. As long as they have enough money in their account to cover their checks, they figure everything is hunky-dory.

Some writers keep no records at all. Others simply toss all receipts, statements, and other bits of financial trivia into a drawer or cardboard box and then at year's end dump it all onto their accountant's desk.

As a result, few writers ever get full credit for their many legitimate expenses, and most wind up paying far more in taxes than is really necessary.

Actually, record keeping is really not difficult at all, and if you can get yourself into the habit of devoting a few minutes each day to updating your records, you'll never have any serious problems. The way to look at it is that keeping adequate records is part of your job, just as sitting down at the typewriter and cranking out copy is. And since you are self-employed, it is up to you to make sure that you follow through. No one else is going to do it for you (unless you have a willing spouse or companion).

We recommend that you keep three separate journals for your expenses—one for entertainment, one for travel, and a third for "other" expenses, such as paper, typewriter ribbons, stamps, etc.

Your books don't have to be historic documents. But they should contain such vital information for each expenditure as the date, amount spent, and the purpose for the expenditure. Put the date at the left, cite your "reasons" in the center, and list the prices at the right for ease of tallying.

It is impossible to get receipts for every single expense, and

Uncle Sam requires only that you keep receipts for expenses of $25 or more (no foolin'). But we suggest you keep as many receipts as humanly possible—even things such as twenty-five-cent tollway slips and the like.

For one thing, when you sit down at day's end to log your expenses, you are apt to forget the little ones without receipts. And second, if you ever are audited, the more receipts you can dump onto the IRS man's desk, the less likely he is to check each one.

These receipts should be separated into three individual piles—one for travel, the second for entertainment, and the third for "other." Then they should be placed into marked envelopes, with a full month's receipts in each category in each envelope. Mark three new envelopes for each new month. This way, should you ever have to locate a particular receipt (such as a phone bill that you paid but the phone company says you didn't pay), you can track it down relatively easily.

Your accountant won't have to refer to your receipts unless he finds a discrepancy in your figures. So once you file them, you won't have to look at them again, unless you get audited.

One final comment on keeping records for all expenses. Although the IRS doesn't require receipts for small expenses, it *does* require documentation. Your expense logs will suffice, and that is another big reason for maintaining them.

Now, getting back to the three main categories of deductible expenses, exactly what comes under each?

Travel

Just about any expenses incurred while on a business trip can be deducted as travel costs. For example, the obvious ones are things such as air fare, car rental, railroad tickets. Not so obvious is that you can deduct the expense whether you go tourist or first class.

In the case of auto expense, there are two methods for arriving at your allowable expenses. One way is by the mile (check with your accountant or the IRS to learn the current allowable cost per mile). The second method is to deduct a percentage of your total auto expense for the year, based on how much you use your car for business. (This involves a "guesstimate," and unless you are really out of line, chances are the IRS won't challenge your figures.)

Lodging expenses are also deductible as travel expenses, and it doesn't matter whether you stay in one of those bargain basement special motels or the finest in the area. About the only way you might raise the IRS man's hackles is if you stayed in the presidential suite or try to write off the total amount even when traveling with a friend, spouse, or paramour.

As for meals, the same rule applies here—all meals, including snacks, are deductible when you are traveling on business. But with President Carter's recent "crackdown" on freewheeling spenders, you should avoid buying drinks for the house and then deducting it.

Tips are another legitimate expense, and here you almost never have a receipt to show how much you left, so it is strictly your word on the matter, unless you use credit cards, in which case the tip may be paid with credit just like the meal.

By the way, waiters and waitresses are becoming aware of the fact that you can pretty much write off any amount, so one of their favorite tricks is to hand you a blank receipt and suggest that you can put in any amount you wish. Or they may simply ask how much you'd like them to make your receipt for. If you just can't figure out why they are being so generous, think again. (They're looking for a fatter tip!)

What about other expenses you incur while traveling on business? Well, if you take in a movie, or stop for a drink after dinner, you can legitimately write the cost off. Health facilities fees, massage fees, greens fees, and many other such costs can also be deducted.

Entertainment

Yes, the cost of entertaining business associates is legally deductible, as long as your log indicates the nature of the client or customer relationship and the need for the entertainment. As a free-lance writer, you can entertain potential sources of information, editors and publishers of magazines with which you deal, and any other persons you can make a case for courting as a writer.

Writing off such lavish expenses as season tickets to pro football or basketball games, the cost of a cabin cruiser, a golf club membership, and similar expenses is allowable, at least theoretically. The catch is that you have to prove that such expenses really were business related. And you can bet that the IRS man with a wife and three kids and a mortgage on a cracker box in the suburbs is going to grit his teeth and prepare to do battle if he spots these items in your return.

Other Expenses

As a free-lance writer you would be surprised to learn just how many of your expenses are deductible, from phone calls to any special equipment you need to pursue your craft. This can range from a slide viewer to tape recorder to telephone answering machine to magazine subscriptions. And in the case of equipment, not only is it deductible but you can also take an investment tax credit on it.

Briefly, the investment tax credit is a flat decrease in your taxes of 10 percent of the cost of such equipment, over and above the regular tax deduction for purchase of the equipment. Where the deduction simply lowers your taxable income, the investment tax credit is worth much more for most writers because it is a direct decrease in the amount of tax paid.

We discussed cameras and related equipment earlier when dealing with the subject of photojournalism. One reason so many free-lance magazine writers carry the very best camera gear is that it is deductible *and* eligible for the 10 percent investment tax credit. In effect, Uncle Sam is helping to subsidize the purchase of the camera gear.

Where must you draw the line on deductible expenses? Well, if you are doing an article on what it's like to participate in a sports car rally, we wouldn't suggest purchasing a new Jaguar with the idea of writing it off. But if you specialize in a particular field and need certain equipment to do your articles, you might be able to get these deductions past.

The best rule to follow when in doubt is to check with your accountant.

The Home Office

In a word, they're deductible for free-lance writers, assuming that you actually do your writing at home. If 20 percent of your home is occupied by you for your office, then you can deduct 20 percent of your rent or mortgage payment. But you must use the office 100 percent for business, and not as an occasional guest room as well, in order to deduct it.

8
Getting "into the Business"

Getting your start as a free-lance writer isn't as difficult as you might imagine. Yes, the competition can be fierce, but what separates the men from the boys is not so much talent as it is drive and perseverance. It's a lot like the story of the tortoise and the hare. The tortoise always seems to be way behind, but when the race concludes, he is the winner.

The biggest problem with most newcomers to the free-lance writing game is that they are too easily discouraged. Rejection slips don't necessarily mean that your material is bad, but it does mean that you either approached the wrong magazine(s) or you took the wrong approach.

What made Henry Ford the greatest industrialist of our time is not that his product was superior. (The Model T was actually a rather primitive beast, even when compared with other cars of its day.) But he was able to mass produce it and sell it at a price that everyone could afford. In short, he determined what the public wanted and then gave it to them.

How does this apply to you as a free-lance magazine writer? Simple. If you are able to put your finger on the pulse of the reading public and determine what subjects people are interested in reading more about, you'll be a winner, simply because your material will be hitting the bull's-eye instead of veering off target.

It should be remembered that the general public is better educated than ever before, and that means they want their magazines to be more sophisticated in the material offered, television notwithstanding. This means that you, the writer, must be better informed as well and able to incorporate your knowledge into your articles in a way that is easily understood.

Established free-lance writers no longer hold the advantage over newcomers to the writing game that they once did. With more magazines than ever before gobbling up available articles at an ever increasing rate, editors are scrambling to find good material. If you can produce, you'll be able to sell your articles. The key lies in being able to keep on top of constantly changing attitudes and interests among the reading public. The market is in a continual state of flux—if you don't keep ahead of things, you'll get left behind.

Go for It!

Hot dog skiers, the acrobats of the winter world, have a saying they use for spurring each other on during competition—"Go for it!" Translated, it means not to hold back but to give it all you've got. This strategy can work for the new writer, too.

If your story is good enough, why not sell it to a top magazine rather than an obscure one. It is just as easy to do research for an article for *Ladies Home Journal* or *Playboy* as it is to research an article for *Model Airplane Monthly,* and it doesn't take too much guessing to figure which of these magazines pays the best.

Likewise, you should adopt the same "go for it" attitude

when it comes to choosing subject matter. How do you know you can't get that interview with Robert Redford when he's in town unless you try?

Remember, even the biggest of big shots was once a newcomer to his own field trying to get a break, just like you. Your chances of getting to see him are just as good as any other writer's. Often it is the writer with the most "chutzpah" or nerve who gets the interview.

As a friend of ours who makes a habit of getting interviews and stories from the biggest names in show business is fond of saying, "The bigger they are, the nicer they are."

Should You "Take the Plunge"?

A big question facing free-lance writers who are just getting started is whether or not to quit their regular jobs to devote full time to writing and selling articles. After all, as much as you want to make writing your profession, there is no guarantee that you will be good enough to make a living out of it. Besides, most writers write primarily because it is fun and a big boost to their egos, and not necessarily because they want to get rich quick.

While the ideal way to approach writing is to go at it full time, few can afford the luxury of taking the plunge with monthly bills rolling in and "baby needing new shoes." So let's assume that you are going to do your writing in your spare time. Your problem now is how to find that free time. As anyone who ever tried to complete a do-it-yourself project knows, events have a way of popping up out of the blue and eating away your precious free time.

The answer is that you must make the time, if writing is really to be important to you. Woodward and Bernstein wrote the book *All the President's Men* between reporting assignments for the *Washington Post*. Joseph Wambaugh wrote *The New Centurions* between shifts when he was a cop. So don't say it can't be done—it can. Just don't wait around hoping for that little light bulb in your head (inspiration) to light up, or you'll never write anything.

Writers are the first to tell you that the toughest thing they do is force themselves to produce a certain amount of material, whether they are in the mood or not. To paraphrase another old cliche, "Writing is 98 percent perspiration and 2 percent inspiration." Or, as we're fond of saying ourselves when people ask how we actually write our articles and books, "The way to write something is to put a sheet of paper in the typewriter and start typing."

Maybe a handful of novelists can afford the luxury of sitting in the south of Spain for six months or a year waiting for their ideas to gell, but the rest of us have to grind it out day in and day out. Like any other job, there are plenty of times when you'd rather be golfing, but you go to work anyway.

There are two basic types of individuals in this world—talkers and doers. Successful free-lance article writers are doers. They manage to find time each day before or after their other jobs or responsibilities to write. You have to learn how to go into your office or study, shut the door, and get down to business. Unplug the phone so it won't ring. Let someone else answer the door with instructions that you aren't home to anyone—even your dear old mother.

It may take a while to get your family adjusted to the fact that when you are writing, you are writing and doing nothing else. But after a few weeks of seeing that you really mean it, they'll accept the situation.

If you have a hard time keeping your nose to the old grindstone, give yourself some incentives—like promising yourself a vacation in Florida or on the ski slopes at Aspen with all the money you'll be making from selling your articles. Or promise yourself that you'll buy that sailboat you always dreamed of skippering with the profits from your writing. Then, whenever the blahs hit, take five and think about your special bonus. Chances are you'll have a much easier time getting yourself psyched up again.

Other Ways to "Psyche" Yourself Up

Analyze some of your better writing and see if you can remember when you produced it. You will probably discover that, like most other writers, there are certain times of the day or night when your creative juices are flowing best. If that is the case, try to arrange your schedule so that you can devote this time to writing instead of other activities.

Another good suggestion is to make sure that you have all necessary tools of your trade when you sit down at the typewriter. This includes a dictionary, a copy of *Roget's College Thesaurus,* typewriter correction tape or fluid, carbon paper, typing paper, and whatever else you require. Nothing can break your train of thought when writing faster than stopping for five minutes while you track whatever you need down.

If something interrupts you at a critical moment, there is no retrieving it later. The spell has been broken.

Speaking of writing tools, one of the most important of all is your outline. Make sure it is in front of you whenever you sit down to work on an article. Your outline is like a blueprint for a carpenter—you may deviate from it occasionally, but without it as a guide you're liable to create a monster.

One of our own favorite tricks for keeping on schedule with articles is to set deadlines for ourselves and then stick to them come hell or high water. For example, if we decide to produce two pages of copy for a particular article on a given day, we do it! If we have only two hours in which to write, we crank out those two pages in record time if we must.

You probably think that such an approach will result in second-rate work. Not at all! For one thing, it is always easier to go back later and edit or revise than it is to do a first draft. And second, if you ask any writer whose background includes reporting for a newspaper, where deadlines come at you several times each day, he'll tell you that some of his best stuff was cranked out as fast as he could type and with an impatient city editor hovering over him.

The master himself, Ernest Hemingway, is said to have written *The Old Man and the Sea* in a single sitting. He knew what he wanted to say, and once he got wound up, there was no stopping him.

Tackle Tough Stories

Unless you regularly force yourself to "upgrade" your reporting and writing skills, you will never improve past a certain point. The best way to upgrade is to tackle articles that you think are too difficult for you to handle. You may fall on your face now and then, but you will also surprise yourself by producing some really outstanding work.

Besides, writers who let themselves fall into a comfortable niche will type themselves in much the same way that actors become typecast by playing the same kind of role over and over. After a while the editors you deal with regularly will peg you as having limited skills, or being "written out." When that happens, you'll find it more and more difficult to sell story ideas, and you'll find that editors call you with assignments less and less.

From a psychological standpoint, forcing yourself to tackle untried fields is good for your character. In a sense, you will be like athletes who continually strive for bigger and better marks as a way of improving themselves.

When you do find yourself occasionally lapsing into the blahs and our other remedies don't work, try rapping with other writer friends. Sometimes it is good to get your problems off your chest. And you may be surprised to discover that other writers are facing the same kind of problems that you are, and suddenly you don't feel so overwhelmed or alone.

9

The Bottom Line

The bottom line for the free-lance writer of articles for magazines is getting paid for your efforts. As we said earlier, you may be in this business strictly for the money, or you may find writing fulfilling in other ways. But without getting paid for our work, there'd be no way of keeping score on how well we're doing compared with other writers and compared with our own previous efforts.

Unfortunately, some writers assume a docile, subservient posture when it comes to selling their articles. And that's bad for the individual as well as the rest of us. Ask any successful salesman how he feels about calling on potential customers, and he'll say that he never feels like he's imposing on anyone. He believes in the value of his product or service, and so he is really doing the contact a favor by exposing him to that product or service.

This is how you should feel about your own work. You should never feel like you are imposing on an editor by sending a query or an article on speculation. After all, he needs writers like you. Without access to a wide variety of freelance articles, he'd either have to beef up his own editorial staff significantly (at great expense) or fold up his tent.

As for remuneration, writing is a skill and an art, and as such it deserves to be rewarded as such. With bus drivers in Chicago earning almost $9 an hour, and plumbers in some parts of the country earning as much as $15 an hour, shouldn't you earn at least this much, if not a good deal more?

Let's say that you spend two hours digging up articles and books in the library, and you spend another two hours skimming this material for additional background information. Finally, you spend another four hours writing and polishing your article and an hour dropping your film off for processing, writing your cover letter, addressing your envelopes, etc. How does all this stack up?

Time spent covering race	5 hours
Library research	2 hours
Reading time	2 hours
Writing time	4 hours
Miscellaneous chores	1 hour
Total time	14 hours
x $7.50/hour	$105.00
Additional cost (phone, gas, film, paper, stamps, etc.)	+ 10.00
Total estimated value of article	$115.00

Now let's say that in his response to your article and letter, the editor of the regional boating magazine indicates that he pays a flat five cents per word, plus $15 for each photo used. After editing your article and trimming it slightly to fit a layout, it comes to 1,800 words; additionally, he plans to use three of your photos at $15 each.

1,800-word article at 5 cents/word	$90.00
3 color photos at $15 each	45.00
Total payment	$135.00

Based on your own evaluation of your story and photos, this magazine is offering you a good price. Of course, if you are a more experienced writer, you might set your hourly worth at $10 or $15 an hour, or even higher, in which case, it wouldn't pay to sell the article to this particular magazine at the price offered. But as an experienced writer, you will probably be able to complete the story in much less time than the beginner, so based on your hourly worth, you might be in the ballpark after all.

In any event, what should your next move be when after evaluating the worth of your article, you get a reply from a magazine that offers less? You have two options:

1. Write or call back, indicating that you have a good deal of time and effort involved in the article and you require X dollars more in order to be able to sell it. The magazine editor will either say yes or no, depending on his evaluation of the piece and his own budget restrictions.

2. If he says no, you can either back water and sell for his price or refuse the offer and try to sell the article and photos to another boating magazine. In this case, you may have to invest some additional time to tailor the article for the new magazine.

The obvious risk is that you will turn down the first offer and then perhaps not be able to sell the article elsewhere for as much or more money. It's all a matter of value. If you really need the money, or if you are anxious to get those by-line articles for your portfolio of writing samples, sell your stuff whenever and wherever you can, regardless of price.

On the other hand, if you are confident that your work is worth what you say it is, and you don't want to sell yourself short, accept the fact that occasionally you'll have to "eat" a story.

How Magazines Pay

For starters, magazines may pay by the word, by the line of type, by the typewritten page, or by the article. While most pay by the word, you will find many, large and small alike, that have their own methods of calculating the price to be paid for articles.

In some cases the magazine has a standard rate, and it pays that for any and all articles, regardless of special content or the author. But more often the magazine will pay over its regular rates to get an article by a well-known writer or personality or to get an exclusive article. (So when you come up with a real exclusive, be sure to hold out for more money.)

In dealing with magazines you will soon discover that their rates vary widely, from as little as a penny a word up to twenty cents a word or more, or from as little as $5 per article up to $5,000 or more. (These are rare indeed, so don't get your hopes up.) The vast majority of articles go for prices of $50 to $500.

As for photos, you will find that black-and-white glossy photos usually go for $5 to $25, while color slides usually go for $25 to $400 or more, depending on the content and the planned use. Color slides often are selected for use on full-color covers, in which case they are obviously worth a good deal more to the magazine.

Unless otherwise specified, magazines purchase full rights to articles and photos when they buy them from you. If you wish to retain second and additional rights, so state in your correspondence. Unless the content of your article is of the sensational or exclusive nature, most editors will go along with your request, as long as you assure them that they will get first publication rights plus the right to reprint the article later if desired.

Do you need a contract? No. If magazine editors sent out contracts for each story they purchased, they'd spend all their time bogged down in paperwork. Editors aren't in business to rip off unsuspecting writers. Although misunderstandings do occur, they are rare indeed, so if an editor tells you he will buy a story for a given price, trust him to pay that price.

Unless otherwise specified, payment is made upon publication of the article. And since most magazines operate on deadlines that are as much as six months ahead of publication dates, you will often have to wait quite a while for your money.

If the magazine appears with your article and you don't receive payment promptly, you should not hesitate to call or write the editor and ask for payment. Oversights do occur for a variety of reasons, and your nudge will usually get quick results.

Remember that the editor liked your article enough to buy it. That means he will welcome other articles and story ideas. And he certainly doesn't want to alienate you by forgetting to pay you for your work. Chances are he will welcome your reminder.

Should you use an agent to represent you in selling your work? No. Agents are usually geared toward promoting authors of book-length manuscripts. They work at a relatively slow pace, and many just aren't as enthusiastic as you are about your own work. In addition, magazine editors are used to dealing directly with writers, while book publishers prefer to deal with an intermediary (the agent).

Finally, agents usually get from 10 percent to 15 percent of the fee for anything of yours they sell. And in the case of a magazine article that sells for a few hundred dollars or less, he won't make enough to justify his really beating the bushes for you, and you aren't getting enough to be able to cut out 15 percent or so and still have the payment be worth your own efforts.

Taking Assignments

As you become established with a number of magazines, you may find that editors begin to call you with story assignments. This is a compliment because it says that your work is well received and, in addition, the editor feels that you can handle the assignment within the time allowed *and* represent his magazine well.

Whether you should take assignments is strictly up to you. Some free-lance writers feel that taking regular assignments is practically the same as going on the payroll. They feel it restricts their own creativity and freedom of movement.

But regular assignments are a blessing to many a free-lance writer who is struggling to make it. And it is another way of getting exposure for your writing talent. Remember, most editors of magazines devour as many other magazines as possible each month in an effort to get fresh ideas for stories and layouts *and* to find promising writers such as you. As far as we're concerned, the more your by-line appears in print, the easier it will be for you to sell your articles—so when a free-lance assignment comes your way, take it!

Should you ever refuse an assignment because you don't think the quality of the magazine in question is worthy of your writing talents? Hell, no. Remember, the bottom line in the writing game is how much you earn during a given period. Even the best writers often publish in obscure or less-than-first-rate publications.

Besides, editors will forget that your story appeared in a second-rate magazine, but they will remember your name, especially as it begins to appear at the top of articles in many quarters. And recognition is what will help you sell your work easier and for more money.

Conclusion

When we wrote this book, we had two purposes in mind. First, we wanted to convince you that becoming a successful free-lance writer of articles for magazines can be a very real possibility for you. Second, we wanted to provide concrete ideas and suggestions, plus a step-by-step plan for researching, writing, and selling magazine articles.

We are among the first to admit that there is no single right way to accomplish a goal, whatever it may be. And we don't presume to say that everything we say is indisputable. Every successful free-lance writer has his own formula for success.

Some of the suggestions we make may not work for you. Others will. But at least after reading this book, you have a pretty good idea of what the world of the free-lance magazine writer is like and how to go about joining the fraternity.

So, if you are ready to give it a try, don't procrastinate. Start your writing career right now. And we'll look forward to seeing your by-line in print soon.

Appendix

In a recent book on the special requirements of writing a column, we devoted a chapter to subject matter. While the list we presented was designed to help people zero in on a particular area of interest for a regular column, it can also be used by the free-lance magazine writer as an "idea file." Here is an abbreviated and slightly altered version of that list:

Accidents—How to avoid them; first-aid methods; statistics on causes.
Agriculture—The state of farming today; how to grow your own vegetables; specialized articles for farm journals.
Animals—Caring for pets; animal "anecdotes"; vanishing species.
Architecture—Trends in home, commercial construction; possibilities for solar heat; saving landmark buildings.
Armed Forces—Whether the "volunteer" Army is working; readiness of reserves; what happens to "old soldiers."

Arms—With more than a million members of the NRA and eight million hunters, plus forty million other gun owners, possibilities for articles are almost endless.

Art—New developments in art; collecting for fun and profit.

Astronomy—With the space age in full swing, stories about any aspect of astronomy have great potential.

Authors—Review of new books; comparison of contemporary authors with the masters; anecdotes.

Automation—This is also the age of automation, and articles about all aspects are potentially big sellers. (Ex.: the home computer center.)

Automobiles—Racing; how-to repair articles; pricing guides; consumer information.

Aviation—A plane in every garage; safety of small versus large planes; how difficult it is to learn to fly.

Babies—Overwritten subject area, plus usually requires medical background.

Bachelor Life—How-to ideas; dispelling myths about swinging singles.

Baseball—Like all sports, it has been worked to death.

The Bible—With upsurge in interest in "Born again" Christians and religion in general, anything unusual, or fresh, will sell.

Bicycling—How to; where to; etc.

Bird Watching—How to get involved.

Blind People—Any news or ideas will sell easily.

Books—See "Authors."

Boy Scouting—How has Scouting changed? First-person stories on scouting activities also have possibilities.

Business—Success stories; how to avoid problems; trends in business.

Carpentry—How-to stories still sell in certain magazines.

Celebrities—Any time you come up with a story about celebrities, it is guaranteed to sell.

Child Care—See "Babies."

Children—Stories written for kids are in demand; also changing views of having children, problems with children, etc.

Christmas—Season story ideas on holidays such as Christmas are big sellers, but you must query as early as May or June!
Church—See "Bible."
Clocks—Collecting them; use in decorating; etc.
Clothes—Fashion articles; new fabrics; tips for cleaning.
Clubs—Informative stories on social, fraternal, civic, and other clubs have limited but strong markets.
Coffee—How to brew it; choosing a coffee maker; how to save money buying it.
Coins—Pretty much limited to articles on collecting.
College—Rising costs; expanding vacancies; differences in attitudes today from the 1960s; opinions of value of college education.
Conservation—Articles on any aspect of conservation are being sought by a wide range of consumer magazines.
Contests—Everyone wants something for nothing; which contests offer the best chance; tales of winners and how they fared.
Corporations—See "Business."
Crafts—Always a good seller if you find a new angle for how-to articles.
Crime—Crime prevention stories are overworked, but ghastly stories are in demand by tabloids and special-interest magazines.
Dancing—Disco dance stories are just about guaranteed to sell, especially if you mention John Travolta's name.
Dating—People never tire of articles about the war of the sexes.
Dentistry—See "Babies."
Divorce—See "Dating."
Dogs—Tough to come up with fresh articles.
Do-It-Yourself—See "Carpentry."
Drama—Culture is in vogue, so stories dealing with actors' views, the "smell of the greasepaint," etc. sell well to big city magazines.
Dreams—Leave this one to the shrinks.

Driving—Tips on defensive driving; driving safety statistics; etc.

Drugs—Interviews with addicts have been done ad nauseum but still sell for some reason.

Eating—Story possibilities range from new diets to great restaurants.

Education—Best markets for education stories are city magazines and community newspapers.

Electronics—Highly technical area, but if you talk the lingo and understand it, you can sell a lot of stories to magazines such as *Science Illustrated*.

Employment—Stories about the current status of the job market never get old and always sell well.

Evangelism—See "Bible."

Farming—See "Agriculture."

Fathers—See "Babies."

Films—See "Authors."

Finance—Consumer interest stories dealing with hidden costs, obtaining loans, dealing with collection agencies, etc. have a ready market.

Fishing—Come up with a new way to catch trout or catfish, and your story will sell to the outdoor magazines.

Flowers—Growing them; arranging them; selling them; even eating them.

Folklore—Regional magazines eat this kind of article up.

Food—See "Eating."

Football—See "Baseball."

Fruit—See "Eating."

Furniture—Buying it; repairing it; using it.

Games—New games for kids; games to play that don't cost anything.

Gifts—Stories dealing with unusual gift possibilities sell well, and in a wide variety of markets, from in-flight magazines to women's magazines.

Golf—See "Baseball."

Gossip—Guaranteed to sell, but watch laws of libel and slander.
Government—Attack big government, government spending, or red tape, and your article can't lose.
Happiness—Leave this to the psychiatrists.
Health—Leave this to the doctors.
Heroes—Leave this to the comic books.
History—See "Folklore."
Hobbies—Amazingly strong market for stories about hobbies of all kinds.
Homes—See "Architecture."
Homosexuality—A hot topic, regardless of what you say. Markets abound.
Horses—See "Dogs."
Hunting—See "Fishing."
Illness—See "Health."
Income—Ideas for earning extra income; how to protect income; etc.
Inflation—Ideas for beating inflation are sure sellers in most markets.
Insurance—Find an interesting angle, and it will sell.
Intelligence—Mini IQ tests; changing views; etc.
Jobs—See "Employment."
Labor—Labor stories can't miss in specialty magazines for unions.
Law—Status of legal profession; changes in laws that affect people.
Literature—See "Authors."
Marriage—See "Dating."
Medicine—See "Health."
Motorcycles—Just about any new angle will sell, and not just in the auto and motorcycle magazines either.
Music—If you know enough about this subject to talk intelligently, you can sell all kinds of articles.
Names—What's in a name? Everyone wants to know.

Negroes—See "Homosexuality." (No reflection intended.)
Opera—Some possibilities for articles, but only if you are an expert who can make opera interesting to the masses.
Patents—See "Insurance."
Pets—See "Dogs."
Photography—Great market but highly technical and competitive.
Plants—See "Agriculture."
Poetry—You will have a hard time giving articles about poetry away.
Politics—Worked to death.
Psychiatry—See "Health."
Railroads—Limited markets, but just about anything will sell to the railroad buff magazines.
Real Estate—Just about the hottest article market going.
Records—If you can talk the language of the teenyboppers, you'll sell whatever you write.
Recreation—Where to; how to; new developments.
Religion—See "Bible."
Restaurants—How to find a good one; reports on great ones.
Science—See "Astronomy."
Sports—See "Baseball."
Solar Power—Anything new in this area can't miss with magazines of all sizes and types.
Taxes—Ditto for taxes and how to beat them, especially since Proposition 13.
TV—Unlikely that you will find anything really fresh to say.
Toys—Safety; unusual toys; shopping for toys.
Travel—There are never enough good travel articles, and markets abound.
Vacations—See "Travel."
Wearing Apparel—See "Clothes."
Weather—Everyone talks about the weather, but no one gets tired of reading about what others have to say, either.
Weight Control—See "Eating."
Women—Just about worked to death, what with women's lib.

Index

A

Advertising Age, 6
Alternative publications, 39
American Newspaper Guild, 48
Approach to the article, 30
Arizona Highways, 5
Assignments, 85-86
Ayer (N.W.) Directory, 7, 57

B

Business articles, 43-45
Business publicity, 14
Business Week, 44

C

Cameras, 49-50
Capote, Truman, 38, 39
Card file, 8
Chicago, Illinois, 12
Chicago, 5
Children's articles, 42-43
Chronological organization of material, 31
Circulation, size of, 5-6

City magazines, 5
Closing paragraph, 40
Consumer magazines, 6
Copyright law, 67-68
Cosmopolitan, 40
Country Style, 4
Crain's Chicago Business, 44

D

Daughters of the American Revolution, 6
Deadlines, 56, 60, 79
Dictionary, 79
Direct mail house mailing lists, 22
Directories of magazines, 7-8

E

Editor & Publisher, 66
Editor & Publisher Yearbook, 7
Editors, 57
Entertainment as a tax deduction, 72
Esquire, 40

F

Factual information, 16, 19-25, 30
Fair reporting, 22
Fiction, 40-41
Files
  ideas, 13, 24-25
  magazine, 8
Filter, camera, 50, 51
First-person narrative, 37-38
Forbes Magazine, 44. 45
"For-profit" magazines, 6
Freedom of the press, 66-67

G

"Grabber" headline, 39

H

Headline of article, 39-40
Hobby magazines, 5
Holiday, 41
Home office, 73
Horizontal magazines, 5
Humorous articles, 42

I

Ideas for articles, 8, 9-17
  development of, 14-17
  file, 13, 24-25
  lists, 10-11, 89-94
  local interests, 12-13
  mailing lists, 13-14
  opinions of others, 16
  other publications, 13, 15
Illustrations for article, 12, 23-24

Income tax, 68-73
  entertainment, 72
  travel, 70-71
Interviews, 22-23, 31-37
  art of success, 32-33, 35-37
  note taking, 31, 33-34
  tape recording, 31, 33, 34
Invasion of privacy, 64-67
Investment tax credit, 72-73

K

Kiwanian, 6

L

Lead paragraph, 40
Legionnaire, 6
Lens, camera, 50, 51
Letter writing, 57, 58-59, 60
Libel, 63-64
Library resources, 20
Life, 47
Litigation, 25
Local interests, 12-13
Look, 47

M

Magazine directories, 7-8
Magazine source file, 8
Mailer, Norman, 38, 39
Mailing lists, 13-14
  direct mail houses, 22
Miller, Dr. Arthur, 67
Ms., 4

N

National circulation, 4-5

New Journalism, 38-39
Newspaper morgues, 20-21
Newspaper techniques, 39-40
New York, 5
New York Times, 44
Nonprofit magazines, 6

O

Office at home, 73
Opening paragraph, 40
Opinionated articles, 16
Organization of material, 30, 31, 40
Organizations as sources of information, 14, 23-24
Originality, 11
Outline, 79

P

Packaging the product, 61
Payment, 83-85
Penthouse, 40
Periodical directories, 7-8
Photographic equipment, 49-51, 72-73
Photojournalism, 12, 23-24, 47-52
  equipment, 49-51
  sale of photographs, 84
  submitting photographs, 52
Plagiarism, 11
Playboy, 4, 6, 31, 40
Plimpton, George, 39
Preliminary research of story, 15
Press releases, 13-14
Price of article, 4, 6, 82-83
Princeton Tiger, 6
Privacy laws, 64-67

Pro forma, 10
Public relations firms, 24

Q

Query letters, 55-56, 57-60
Questionnaires, 21-22

R

Rates of payment, 83-85
Reader's Guide to Periodical Literature, 8, 20
Redbook, 40
Reed, Rex, 31
Reference materials, 79
Regional circulation, 4-5
Rejection slips, 56, 75
Researching a story, 15, 19-25
  interviews, 22-23
  newspaper morgues, 20-21
  other articles, 20
  professional organizations, 23-24
  proof of sources, 25
  surveys, 21-22
Rights to publication, 84
Rolling Stone, 4, 39
Rotarian, 6

S

Sandburg, Carl, 12
Science writing, 45-46
Skate Boarder, 5
Slant of article, 30
Slick magazines, 4
Southern, Terry, 39
Sporting News, 4
Sports Illustrated, 4

Sports magazines, 5
Standard Rate and Data Service (SRDS), 7
State magazines, 5
Story ideas, 8, 9-17
   development of, 14-17
   file, 13, 24-25
   lists, 10-11, 89-94
   local interests, 12-13
   mailing lists, 13-14
   opinions of others, 16
   other publications, 13, 15
Style of writing, 29-30
Submitting articles, 17, 55-57, 76
   packaging of, 61
   query letters, 57-60
Submitting photographs, 52
Survey taking, 21-22
Synopsis of article idea, 17

T

Tabloids, 4
Talese, Gay, 39
Tape recorded interviews, 31, 33, 34
Taxes, income, 68-73
   entertainment, 72
   travel, 70-71

Thesaurus, 79
Third-person narrative, 38
Time, 4
Time to write, 77-78
Title of article, 39-40
Town & Country, 41
Trade magazines, 6
Travel and Leisure, 41
Travel articles, 41-42
Travel tax deductions, 70-71

V

Vertical magazines, 5, 6
Village Voice, 39

W

Wall Street Journal, 44
Water Skier, 5-6
Wolfe, Tom, 39
Writer, 7
Writer's Digest, 7
Writer's Market, 7, 57
Writing style, 29-30